ROMANS
The Freedom Letter
VOLUME 1
Romans 1-7

by

ALAN F. JOHNSON

MOODY PRESS

CHICAGO

Library of Congress Cataloging in Publication Data

Johnson, Alan F.
  Romans: the freedom letter.

  Bibliography: p.
  Contents: v. 1. Romans 1-7.
  1. Bible. N.T. Romans—Commentaries. I. Title.
BS2665.3.J63 1984   227 '.107   84-1026
ISBN 0-8024-0446-4   (v. 1)

20

CONTENTS

PREFACE TO THE REVISED EDITION

Since the first draft of this commentary was written, several events have occurred that make the revision desirable. The intervening years have seen the publication of two monumental studies on the book of Romans. C.E.B. Cranfield's two-volume work (see "Selected Bibliography") is a model of careful, conservative, historical exegesis full of valuable insights on Paul's thought in Romans. I have incorporated his materials throughout wherever I thought they were helpful. More recently, Ernst Käsemann's German commentary has been translated into English (see Selected Bibliography). Although not conservative, it is nevertheless a gold mine of information on the epistle. I have likewise referred to this work in the present edition, though less extensively than Cranfield. Equally impressive have been two recent studies on Judaism in the first century: E. P. Sanders's *Paul and Palestinian Judaism* (1977), and M. Hengel's two-volume *Judaism and Hellenism*. These later works have greatly expanded our understanding of the subject.

There has also appeared in recent years the *New International Version* of the Bible (NIV). This book now incorporates and discusses numerous renderings of the new translation.

Further, the evangelical and charismatic resurgence in America of the last decade, not always deeply theological, warrants that a contemporary commentary on Romans should address issues relevant to concerns raised by this phenomenon.

Finally, we must consider the continually changing face of the world. Recently we have seen the rise of Islamic fundamentalism, the growing threat of nuclear holocaust, the continuing problems of the Middle East, and the emergence of the abortion issue and the Moral Majority. Such things call for a fresh look at the message of Paul's great epistle and its contemporary relevance. I hope that those who have found the earlier work helpful will find this revision even more satisfying.

Wheaton, Illinois, 1984

FREEDOM

"Public freedom at last depends on spiritual freedom, and spiritual freedom is not in human nature but in its redemption."

P. T. FORSYTH

THE BOOK OF ROMANS IN ONE SENTENCE

"What is man? Man is God's creature; Yes, but man is God's image, and through the misuse of his God-bestowed freedom, man is God's shame and man is God's problem; But by that incredible strategy of the cross, God makes it possible for man to become the Creator's child; And man may become the Creator's co-laborer, and man, finite man, may become the friend of an infinite and all-holy God; And ultimately man may be, if he will have it so, God's glory."

VERNON C. GROUNDS

To

Rea, Jan, Kris, Lynn, and Lisa—
without whose loving companionship
this book
would have been finished
five years ago

PREFACE TO THE ORIGINAL WORK

Every book must be read in view of its intended purpose if the author's efforts are to be found helpful. This book is not the book of Romans. At best it is a brief attempt to explain and comment on some of Paul's main themes in the letter. As such, it must not be used as a substitute for Paul's own letter, which is far more important than anything we could say about it. You must read and reread the book of Romans itself as you use this commentary. Every reader should have open before him the actual letter of Paul and first read each paragraph section of Romans and then consult the suggested explanation.

These notes are human, fallible, and subject to revision. The aim is not sermonic or devotional but a fresh interpretation of the ageless letter in the light of our contemporary age and its needs.

Though the main body of the book has the college student and the concerned layman in mind, the more important exegetical and theological problems are briefly addressed in the footnotes. Thus there are two books in one.

It has been an inexpressible experience of joy and learning for me to have spent these many hours poring over the rich truths found in Paul's letter to the Romans. This epistle has changed my life. What I have learned of God and myself from the book has definitely affected the whole quality of my life. If even some small spark of this enthusiasm and joy can reach across these pages to the reader, I shall be deeply grateful.

INTRODUCTION

Since the content of the book of Romans is weighty and without much practical personal application until chapter 12, I would like at the outset to stress the great significance of the book lest discouragement over mastering its content turn you away too soon from its inspiring pages.[1]

A few quotations will help put Romans into perspective. Coleridge said of Romans that it was "the profoundest work in existence." Luther remarked that it was "the chief part of the New Testament and the perfect Gospel." "If a man understands it," Calvin stated, "he has a sure road open for him to the understanding of the whole Scripture." Godet referred to it as the "Cathedral of Christian Faith." More recently the notable Princeton scholar Bruce Metzger has called Romans the "Constitution of Universal Christianity."

Great intellects like Augustine, Luther, Calvin, and Edwards have studied Romans only to discover depths beyond their depths. George Wilson of Scotland, the distinguished poet, biographer, and scientist, received Christian instruction

---

1. For a thorough discussion of all the introductory questions pertaining to Romans, among the best sources are Donald Guthrie, *New Testament Introduction,* 3d ed., rev. (Downers Grove, Ill.: Inter-Varsity, 1970), pp. 393ff.; Everett F. Harrison, *Introduction to the New Testament* (Grand Rapids: Eerdmans, 1964), pp. 280ff.; Paul Feine and Johannes Behm, *Introduction to the New Testament,* ed. Werner G. Kümmel, trans. A. J. Matthill, Jr. (Nashville: Abingdon, 1966), pp. 216ff.; C.E.B. Cranfield, *A Critical and Exegetical Commentary on the Epistle to the Romans,* 2 vols., The International Critical Commentary (Edinburgh: T. and T. Clark, 1975, 1979). This last work contains a model study on the history of interpretation of the epistle (1:30-44).

from his friend Dr. John Cairns, who wrote to him of Romans: "The Gospel tide nowhere forms so many deep, dark pools where the neophyte may drown. . . . You will have something like a glimpse of the divine depth and richness of that despised old textbook, the New Testament."[2]

It may be because Romans is the greatest treatise on God that has ever been written that the letter has figured prominently in every significant evangelical renaissance in history.[3] Such was the case with Augustine, Luther, and John Wesley. Although not a full return to evangelical faith, the more recent work of Karl Barth on Romans (*Romerbrief,* 1919) broke the stranglehold of liberal theology on the scholarly world and brought some significant return to a biblical theology.

A book that has been so used by God in days past might also in our day play a role in the awakening of God's people from their slumber. That such a need exists can be abundantly documented. Consider, for example, the timely words of Dr. John A. MacKay, president of Princeton Seminary for twenty-three years:

> It seems increasingly clear that the chief need of contemporary Christianity and of society in general in this confused and revolutionary time is an evangelical renaissance. By that I mean a rediscovery of the Evangel, the Gospel, in its full dimension of light and power, together with the elevation of the Gospel to the status that belongs to the Gospel in the thought, life, and activity of all persons and organizations that bear the name "Christian."[4]

2. Cited by A. Skevington Wood, *Life by the Spirit* (Grand Rapids: Zondervan, 1963), p. 8.
3. Leon Morris, "The Theme of Romans," in *Apostolic History and the Gospel,* ed. Ward Gasque and Ralph Martin (Grand Rapids: Eerdmans, 1970), p. 263.
4. John A. MacKay, "Toward an Evangelical Renaissance," *Christianity Today* 16, no. 9 (February 4, 1972): 6-8. Consider also the recent statement of Jeremy Rifkin, who notes that "the cumulative evidence suggests that the late seventies could, in fact, mark the beginning of a religious revival in America." *The Emerging Order: God in the Age of Scarcity* (New York: Ballantine, 1979), p. 93.

Or consider the starting words of C. Rene Padilla of Buenos Aires, Argentina, who, in reviewing three books on missions in *Christianity Today*, suggested that the important questions they raise can all be reduced to one: "What is the Gospel?"[5]

With this important historical precedent in mind, we can well afford to apply ourselves to the careful study of Paul's letter, expecting that God may in some small measure kindle anew our love and devotion to Him and perhaps enable us to be a part of a new evangelical renaissance in our day.

AUTHOR, DATE, AND PLACE OF WRITING

So conclusive is the argument for Pauline authorship of this epistle that no serious scholar doubts it comes from the noted apostle to the Gentiles. Not only in the great theme of the grace of God, but in the evidence that the person who wrote the letter was without doubt a Jew who was thoroughly familiar with Pharisaical Judaism (Acts 23:6), as well as one who was burdened to minister to the Gentiles (Acts 13:47; Gal. 2:2, 8; see Rom. 11:13), do we have further support for the letter's authorship by Paul?

Although Paul no doubt could identify with the Greco-Roman culture in which he was raised at Tarsus (Acts 22:3) and bear the impress of responsibilities of Roman citizenship (Acts 22:25), the greatest influence on his life was his rabbinic, pharisaical Jewish background (Rom. 11:1; Gal. 1:13-14; Phil. 3:5-6). Today scholars are increasingly convinced that Paul's Jewish background places him squarely in the mainstream Judaism of his day. He was not a cheap or second-class Jew.[6]

---

5. C. Rene Padilla, "What Is the Gospel?" *Christianity Today* 17 (July 20, 1973):1106.
6. See Richard N. Longenecker, *Paul, Apostle of Liberty* (Grand Rapids: Baker, 1976); also W. D. Davies, *Paul and Rabbinic Judaism*, rev. ed. (New York: Harper, 1955).

Other important influences on Paul's life were his acceptance of Jesus as Messiah and Lord (Gal. 1:15-16), his contact with the Christian teaching before him (Gal. 1:18; Rom. 1:3, 4) and his missionary-apostleship calling (Gal. 1:16).

Romans was most probably written in Corinth during Paul's last visit, which lasted about three months, in the spring of A.D. 57 or 58 (Acts 20:1-3).[7] This date depends upon internal references to the apostles' circumstances as they relate to information in the book of Acts. A key factor in the actual year date involves Proconsul Gallio, who heard charges against Paul at Corinth on Paul's second missionary journey (Acts 18:12-18). According to an inscription found at Delphi, Gallio was installed as proconsul at Corinth about A.D. 52. Calculating from this date until Paul finally left Corinth for the last time would involve another five years (Acts 20:1-3).

Recognizing the early date of the book of Romans as probably occuring before any of the written gospels adds importance to its portrait of Christianity.

OCCASION AND PURPOSE

Paul apparently had finished his work in the east, and after depositing the collection for the poor saints in Jerusalem, he plans to visit Rome on his way to Spain (15:22-28). The apostle, in hopes that the important Roman church might be an aid to his missionary endeavors in the far west, therefore wanted to introduce himself and give a sample of his message to the saints in Rome before he arrived. But does this account for the lengthy and intricate explanation of his gospel message that the letter contains? Why not send a brief note through Phoebe (16:1) and indicate that he would give a full verbal statement of his message when he arrived in Rome?

One explanation of the long, weighty letter might be that he expected trouble in Jerusalem that could prevent him from ever reaching Rome. The treatise, then, would provide a final

7. Guthrie, p. 25.

memorial to his ministry and a basis for the Roman church to evangelize the west in his absence.[8]

Another intriguing view involves an attempted historical reconstruction of the church situation in Rome in A.D. 57. Both from Acts 18:2 and external evidence, we know that the emperor Claudius issued an edict evicting all the Jews from Rome in A.D. 49 due to disturbances over Christ (see note 10 in Chapter 1). The thirteen or so Jewish synagogues in Rome at the time lacked any central leadership, and the members were quite culturally diverse. When the Christian mission came to Rome, some synagogues were receptive, whereas others were negative. In the aftermath of the clash between synagogues over the Christ issue, the whole Jewish population (40-50,000) was required to leave Rome. This marked the end temporarily of the Jewish-Christian presence in Rome. At that time (A.D. 49), house churches were formed so that the Christians could meet apart from the synagogue. During the five years the edict was in effect (until the beginning of Nero's reign), the house churches did not have Jewish-Christians. However, when the Jews returned to Rome, they found the church different from the way they knew it in the synagogue context. There was now a Gentile majority, and they were in leadership. The book of Romans, then, in this view was written to the Gentile majority to exhort them to welcome and to live together in one congregation with the Jewish-Christian minority.[9]

More certain is the fact that there is a strong emphasis in the letter on Paul's view of salvation versus certain legalistic Jewish concepts and the integrity of his gospel over against

8. Harrison, p. 286.
9. Wolfgang Wiefel, "The Jewish Community in Ancient Rome and the Origins of Roman Christianity," in *The Romans Debate,* ed. Karl P. Donfried (Minneapolis: Augsburg, 1977), pp. 100-19; similarly Krister Stendahl, "Paul and the Introspective Conscience of the West," in *Paul among Jews and Gentiles* (Philadelphia: Fortress, 1976), pp. 78-96. For a masterful and thrilling historical reconstruction, see historian Paul Maier's *The Flames of Rome* (New York: Doubleday, 1981), especially chap. 7.

alleged charges of moral permissiveness. Paul must expect to find in Rome such objections to the gospel as he customarily preaches it.[10] In any event, Romans provides us, as well as the ancient Italians, with an introduction to some of the main currents in Paul's theological thoughts.

THE ROMAN CHURCH

There is considerable speculation both as to the origin of the church in Rome and its constituency. Nothing is known with certainty, but some general directions may be suggested. Concerning the Roman Catholic view of Peter founding the church, there is no historical evidence. Furthermore, Peter was still in Jerusalem at the time of the Jerusalem Council (Acts 15 c. A.D. 50), yet it is almost certain that Christians were gathering in church homes in Rome before this time (1:7).[11] It is difficult to imagine Paul writing to the church at Rome as he did if Peter indeed had founded it, or why he should omit reference to Peter anywhere in the letter if the fisherman was the apostle in residence in Rome.

A further suggestion explains the origin of the church as arising from Roman Jews who were present in Jerusalem on the day of Pentecost and, having been converted, returned to establish the church (Acts 2:10). However, there is no evidence that any Roman Jews were in fact among the converted at Pentecost. Furthermore, the word "dwelling" in Acts 2:5 (KJV) could also refer to permanent residents *living* in Jerusalem.

Another view, which likewise has no certainty, is that the church was founded by various converts of Paul who had heard his preaching in other parts of the world and were converted and then traveled to Rome for various reasons. Paul certainly knew by name a large number of people at Rome

---

10. Feine and Behm, pp. 221-22; Guthrie, p. 27.
11. Acts 18:2-3 implies that Aquila and Priscilla (Prisca in Rom. 16:3, NASB), who came to Corinth from Rome, were already Christian which would further confirm the earlier existence of the church in Rome before A.D. 49.

(Rom. 16:3-15)—which might support this view. On the other hand, if this is the correct explanation, it is difficult to see why Paul was so anxious to go to Rome to preach the gospel to those who had already heard him before.

Concerning the constituency of the church in Rome, it seems quite evident from the internal references that it consisted mainly of Gentiles with some Jewish intermixture (1:5-8; 1:12-14; 6:19; 11:13; 11:28-31; 15:17; 15:15). Cranfield best summarizes the evidence: "The truth would seem to be that it is impossible to decide with anything like absolute certainty whether at the time Paul wrote to them the majority of the Roman Christians were Gentiles or Jews, and that we ought therefore to leave this question open."[12] It is estimated that the Roman church must have grown to considerable size during Paul's time.[13] This growth may account for the multiple meeting places referred to in the letter (16:5; 14, 15, 16). The frequency of the names mentioned in chapter 16 in the catacombs and other early Roman inscriptions is well documented by C. H. Dodd in his *Epistle to the Romans.*[14]

THEME AND CHIEF CHARACTERISTICS

The theme of Romans can be stated in different ways. Some prefer to call it "salvation as the revelation of God's righteousness"; others, "the righteousness of God by faith"; or "justification by grace through faith"; and "God saving men in Christ." It is all but universally agreed that the theme of Romans finds brief statement in the words of Romans 1:16-17: "For I am not ashamed of the gospel, for it is the power of God for salvation to every one who believes, to the Jew first and also to the Greek. For in it the righteousness of God is revealed from faith to faith; as it is written, 'But the righteous man shall live by faith.' "

This theme of salvation as the righteous act of God accom-

12. Cranfield, 1:21.
13. Guthrie, p. 24.
14. C. H. Dodd, *Epistle to the Romans* (Naperville, Ill. Allenson, 1932).

plished in Jesus Christ's death and resurrection and pro-
claimed in the gospel message is set forth meticulously in
Paul's exposition. He first shows the desperate need of all
men before God for this salvation. Gentiles are seen as
notoriously given over to idolatry and various perversions
that prove their rebellion against the Creator (1:18-32), while
Jews are no better off for their religious heritage because they
have perverted God's grace into self-righteousness (2:1—
3:20). Only God's mighty act of grace and love accomplished
in Jesus Christ's death and resurrection and received freely on
the basis of faith can effect the pardon and reconciliation of
men who are under God's condemnation (3:21—4:25).

Next, Paul unfolds the truth that this new standing before
God also brings into existence a new being realized in the
Christian experience of joy and certainty (5:1-21) and in the
progressive defeat of the rule of sin in one's life through the
power of the indwelling Spirit of Christ (6:1—8:39). After
treating the historical problem of Israel's rejection of the
Messiah and His gospel and Gentile apathy and ignorance
(9—11), he turns to general exhortations concerning specific
areas of Christian living—personal, societal, political, and
fraternal (12:1—15:13).

Among the chief characteristics of the letter are its long introduction, the unusual number of personal greetings at the
close of the letter, more extensive use of the Old Testament in
quotations (about 57 times) than all his other letters com-
bined, and the rich theological emphasis, especially on God
Himself. The most common words in the letter are "God"
(153 times), "law" (72 times), "Christ" (65 times), "sin" (48
times), "Lord" (43 times), and "faith" (40 times).

INTEGRITY OF THE LETTER

The chief critical questions relate to the nature of chapter
16 and the different textual traditions at points in the letter.
The benediction ("the grace of our Lord Jesus Christ be with
you") is placed in chapter 16 either at the end of verse 20
(most witnesses), or at verse 24 (some), or after verse 27

(some). The position of doxology (16:25-27) constitutes the greatest textual problem. We can only summarize the facts and state our conclusion in brief. More interested students should consult lengthier treatments.[15]

Though the doxology appears in many manuscripts after 14:23, and in one early witness after 15:33, and in several texts both after 14:23 and at 16:25, the weight of early evidence favors placing it at 16:25-27.[16] Certainly the doxology is Pauline and relates in content to the epistle of Romans. No serious attention should be given to theories such as the Ephesian destination of chapter 16, or that the original letter ended at 14:23 or 15:33. The theory that traces the varied history of the textual tradition of chapters 15 and 16 to the influence of the early heretic Marcion is probably least open to dispute.[17]

15. Guthrie, pp. 28-41; Cranfield, 1:5-11; John Murray, *The Epistle to the Romans,* 2 vols. (Grand Rapids: Eerdmans, 1959), 2:262-68.
16. Murray, 2:268. Since most of the lectionary texts support the placing of the doxology at 14:23, it may be that the majority of manuscripts were influenced by this tradition.
17. Guthrie, pp. 393ff.; Donfried, pp. 120-48.

OUTLINE OF ROMANS

I. The Opening of the Letter (1:1-17)
   A. The Apostle's Greeting (1:1-7)
   B. Paul and the Romans (1:8-15)
   C. The Theme of His Letter (1:16-17)
II. The Doctrinal Foundation of Christianity: The Gospel According to Paul (1:18—11:36)
   A. Mankind's Condition: Under the Judgment of God (1:18—3:20)
      1. Man without the Knowledge of the Bible (1:18-32)
      2. Man with the Knowledge of the Bible (2:1—3:8)
      3. Conclusion: Moral Guilt of the Whole World (3:9-20)
   B. The Good News: The Gift of Righteousness by Faith (3:21—4:25)
      1. God's Provision: The Gift of Righteousness (3:21-31)
      2. Abraham and Justification by Faith (4:1-25)
   C. The New Situation: Freedom from the Wrath of God (5:1-21)
      1. Benefits Stemming from Freedom from the Wrath of God (5:1-11)
      2. Adam and Christ (5:12-21)
   D. The New Situation: Freedom from Sin's Captivity (6:1-23)
      1. Union with Christ in His Death and Resurrection (6:1-14)
      2. Bondage to Righteousness (6:15-23)
   E. The New Situation: Freedom from the Law's Domination (7:1-25)

1

THE OPENING

1:1-17

Ancient Greek letters in the first century, unlike ours, customarily began with the names of sender and recipient and a short greeting involving thanksgiving to God. Paul expands the usual address in an unusually long and highly significant form to express a brief statement of his Christian faith and his ministry (vv. 1-7) and to relate his genuine concern for those in Rome (vv. 8-17). Paul had not yet visited Rome. It is this fact that explains the length of the introduction—he was zealous to inform the church at Rome of his earnest desire and determination to go there. Since most of the key ideas occurring throughout the remainder of the letter are found in this introduction, we can profitably pay close attention to it in attempting to understand Paul's thought.

The following overall view of the introduction may be helpful to refer back to as the details are discussed.

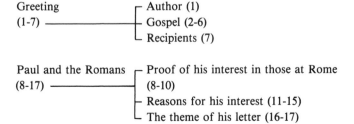

Greeting (1-7) ── Author (1)
Gospel (2-6)
Recipients (7)

Paul and the Romans (8-17) ── Proof of his interest in those at Rome (8-10)
Reasons for his interest (11-15)
The theme of his letter (16-17)

THE APOSTLE'S GREETING

1:1-17

In verses 1-7 Paul identifies and describes himself, relates his calling, gives the essential essence of the gospel, and greets the Roman Christians. Paul, the author, describes himself in verse 1 in a threefold manner. He is first of all a "bond-servant of Christ Jesus." This term occurs as a frequent identification of the followers of Christ in the New Testament (Gal. 1:10; James 1:1; 2 Pet. 1:1; Jude 1). In Greek usage the word "bond-servant"—*doulos*—denotes a slave and would not be used of a Greek citizen's relationship to his ruler or divine king. Although it is possible that Paul could be thinking of serving Jesus Christ as an actual slave in the Greek or Roman sense, it is more likely that he had the Semitic idea of a slave in mind. The Hebrew kings could be served, and the highest of his ministers might be regarded as his slaves (1 Sam. 8:11-14). Distinguished members and citizens of the theocratic kingdom of Israel were also called the servants of God (2 Sam. 7:19, Amos 3:7). Paul, then, appears as an outstanding member and chief minister, or slave, of God in His new divine program.

Second, he refers to himself as (divinely) "called *as* an apostle." Again, Paul's idea probably goes back to the Rabbinic Jewish usage of "apostle" (Gk. *apostolos;* Heb. *shaliah*) as a term to denote one who is legally authorized to act as the representative or proxy of another and who carries the full authority of the one who commissions him.[1] Thus Paul claims direct divine authority as a validly commissioned representative of Jesus Christ Himself (Gal. 1:11-12). One should not, then, hesitate in accepting the teaching of Paul as having anything less than the very authority of Christ Himself.

Third, Paul declares himself to be "set apart for the gospel of God." He may have the calling of the prophets of old in

---

1. G. Kittel and G. Friedrich, eds., *Theological Dictionary of the New Testament* (Grand Rapids: Eerdmans, 1964), 1:415. (This reference is hereafter referred to as TDNT.)

mind (Jer. 1:5) as he relates his peculiar experience of having God mark him out as a special missionary to the Gentiles (Acts 13:1-2; Gal. 1:15). He was set apart "for the gospel of God," that is, in order to proclaim it. Paul's word for gospel, *euangelion,* should be translated "good news" (i.e., something good has happened) to bring out its full sense.[2] It is this gospel, or message, of God's salvation that burdens Paul's heart throughout the whole letter (1:1, 9, 15, 16).

In verses 2-6 Paul digresses briefly from his greeting to dwell upon the essential subject of the good news, "Jesus Christ our Lord" (v. 4). For his Jewish readers he is especially eager to state that this gospel has historical continuity with God's revelations to Israel in the promises given through the prophets in the Old Testament (Rom. 3:21, 31; 4:6; Luke 24:25-27, 44-47; 1 Pet. 1:10-12). "Scripture" designates the officially recognized body of Temple writings that were considered divinely originated (inspired) and thus authoritative for teaching and conduct (2 Tim. 3:15-16). "Holy" (only used here of Scripture) further emphasizes its source as distinctively *divine* revelation (3:2; 9:17; 15:4).

Paul now proceeds to identify the substance of his gospel as that which pertains to God's Son, Jesus Christ, who as true man and true God in one mysterious being bestows upon him whatever grace and authority he possesses (vv. 3-5). Here in two lines of antithetical parallelism (vv. 3-4) one finds a brief statement of the unique person of Jesus of Nazareth.[3]

First, in respect to his real humanity ("according to the

2. Cranfield (*A Critical and Exegetical Commentary on the Epistle to the Romans,* 1:55) shows that the word has connections to the Old Testament, where it means either to announce good news, especially of victory (e.g., 1 Sam. 31:9), or to announce the inbreaking of God's reign, the advent of His salvation, vengeance, or vindication (e.g., Pss. 40:9; 96:2; Isa. 40:9). There are connections also to the pagan world, where the word was used of the emperor-cult to announce such events as the birth of an heir, his coming of age, and His accession. Paul's use would contrast with the latter since he speaks of the good news *of God.*

3. It is quite probable that in these two verses Paul is making use of an already existing Christian confessional formula (Cranfield 1:57). There are possibly three similar passages in Romans (3:24-26; 10:9-10; 16:25b-26).

flesh''), Jesus was born a Jew (descended from Abraham) in the family line of David (Matt. 1:6; Luke 3:31; Acts 2:30; Rev. 5:5). Although Paul does not dwell upon the actual historical facts of Jesus' life on earth, it is evident that he nevertheless considered that real historical life (as the gospels relate) to be of the utmost importance to the validity of the gospel he preaches. He taught what the gospels later confirmed, that according to the Old Testament (2 Sam. 7:16) and Jewish belief, the Messiah would be from Davidic descent.[4]

Yet something else must be said about Jesus, not contradictory to His true humanity but complementary. "According to the flesh" in verse 3 stands in parallel to "according to the Spirit" in verse 4. Although the expression "Spirit of holiness" may be a reference to the Holy Spirit,[5] many commentators feel it is more appropriate to understand this expression as a reference either to Christ's divine personality, which would, because of the parallelism, form a complement to the previous expression about His human nature, or to His human spirit, distinguished by an exceptional holiness.

The church has always taught that though the life Jesus lived on earth was wholly human, the personality revealed was God, the Son of the Father. It must be stressed that without this truth of the dual character of Jesus, not only is our concept of God affected, but the gospel becomes pointless.[6]

4. Daily in the synagogues today the fifteenth and seventeenth benedictions of the ancient Jewish prayer known as the *Shemoneh Esreh* (Eighteen Benedictions) refers to the expectation of the coming of a Davidic Messiah: "Speedily cause the offspring of David, thy servant, to flourish . . . may our remembrance ascend . . . with the remembrance of our fathers, of Messiah the son of David thy servant. . . ." These two prayers were formulated well before the birth of Jesus.

5. Cranfield (1:64) holds this position and argues that the "Holy Spirit, who as given by the exalted Christ, is the manifestation of His power and majesty, and so the guarantee of His having been appointed Son of God in might."

6. Donald Baillie, *God Was in Christ* (New York: Scribner's, 1948), pp. 144ff. contains a worthwhile discussion of how the trinitarian concept of God among Christians uniquely advances a concept of God as a God of grace.

The word "declared" in the Greek (*horizo*) is related to our English word "horizon," which "defines" or "delimits" the boundary between the sky and the earth. The early church Fathers taught that in God's powerful deed of raising Jesus from the dead there lies irrefutable evidence clearly to mark out or distinguish this human life as the divine Son of God and hence rightfully and solely our *Lord*. Recent interpreters argue that the expression means that by the resurrection Christ was "appointed" Son-of-God-in-power (in contrast to His being Son of God in apparent weakness and poverty in His earthly life).[7]

It is from this person that Paul claims to have received grace (gifts of enablement) and apostleship (commission as an ambassador) for the purpose of everywhere securing men to put their trust wholly in Christ and be obedient to Him. His mission for the sake of Christ's name (i.e., for Christ Himself) brings him into contact with those at Rome who are Jesus Christ's called ones like Paul himself.

Finally, in verse 7 he finishes the address by referring to the recipients in their earthly status as Romans and in their relation to God as loved by Him (for Christ's sake) and called to a life of separation unto God as saints. They are not "called to be saints," not "called because saints" but "saints (holy) because called" (Augustine). "The holiness is not primarily that of individual moral character, but that of consecration to God's service." Sainthood is "therefore ascribed to all Christians, who are, however, bound by this very consecration to personal holiness of life."[8] As "saints" they are to be separated from the world's values and consecrated wholly for God's use. "Grace" was customarily used in Greek letter addresses, whereas "peace" (Heb. *shalom*) was and still is the common greeting among Semitic peoples (Num. 6:24-26). Paul enriched these standard terms with added Christian significance.

Having now introduced his letter, himself, and his gospel

7. Cranfield, 1:62.
8. E. H. Gifford, "Romans," in *The Bible Commentary: New Testament* (New York: Scribner's, 1881), 3:57.

(vv. 1-7), he will go on to explain further his interest in the Romans and the full meaning of God's good news.

PAUL AND THE ROMANS

1:8-15

In verses 8-17 Paul briefly relates his own genuine personal concern for those in Rome, giving proof of his feelings in his thankfulness for their faith (v. 8), in his unceasing remembrance of them in prayer (v. 9), and in his unrelieved desire to visit them and labor among them in preaching the gospel that he briefly summarizes (vv. 10-17).

Paul's thanksgiving to God (v. 8) reveals not only his own large heart of love, since many of those addressed were probably not his own converts, but also the virility of their witness to Christ in the non-Christian communities. "Your faith" would not mean "the Christian faith which you hold in common with all other Christians," but rather "the Christian faith *as* you hold it.'"[9] Their zeal for Christ and their love for one another was so manifested that others announced everywhere that something had happened to the Romans (1 Thess. 1:6-8).[10] This confirms Jesus' words that a city built on a mountain cannot be hid (Matt. 5:14).

In his prayer and earnest desire to visit them he offers another proof of his sincere concern for their welfare (vv. 9-15). Note the expression, "serve in my spirit" (v. 9). His service consisted not merely in outward activity but more

9. C. K. Barrett, *The Epistle to the Romans* (New York: Harper & Row, 1957), p. 24.

10. This testimony becomes more meaningful when it is remembered that according to the Roman historian Suetonius, the emperor Claudius had forced the Jews out of Rome in A.D. 49 (Acts 18:2) because of "trouble instigated under the influence of Chrestus" (*Lives of the Twelve Caesars* [New York: Random House, Mod. Lib., n.d.], chap. 25). "Chrestus" is probably a mispelling for Christus (Christ), and the disturbances were probably caused by the agitation and rivalry between Christians and Jews in the synagogues of Rome as Christ was preached as Messiah and Lord (C. K. Barrett, ed., *The New Testament Background: Selected Documents* [New York: Macmillan, 1957], p. 14); Paul Maier, *The Flames of Rome,* chap. 7.

significantly in the service of worship to God in his inner man that issued forth in the outward labor of preaching the gospel of His Son. "If perhaps now at last by the will of God" (v. 10) reflects the delicate, beautiful, and important relationship between praying expectantly to God for a specific matter and at the same time recognizing a submission to the will of God, knowing that what we earnestly desire may not be His will, at least at the present. Paul desires that by his coming and ministry the Holy Spirit would so use him that the Romans would receive the benefit of the presence and power of God (v. 11), yet not themselves only but—in a beautiful touch of humility—that Paul himself also might be mutually strengthened in the practice of his faith by his interaction with them in this service (v. 12; 1 Cor. 12:7).

It may be asked why Paul, if he was so eager to come to Rome, had not come before this. He answers by further assuring them of his love, explaining that he had repeatedly attempted to come, but in each former case he had been prevented (Rom. 15:22-23). Paul was the author of his purposes but not of his circumstances (v. 13). He did not have a constant, unending series of successes!

Another reason for his burden to preach especially to the Romans relates to the universal character of the gospel message (vv. 14-15). Because of Paul's calling he was morally obligated to minister the gospel to all men without respect to their culture or social status. "Greeks . . . barbarians . . . wise . . . foolish" (v. 14) refers to those inhabitants of the regularly recognized Greek city-states (Greeks, "wise") and those outside these areas (barbarians, "foolish") such as the Gauls, Scythians, Celts, and Spaniards, who were considered by the Greeks as uncultured in that they were unable to speak Greek clearly (1 Cor. 14:11). Thus, because the relation in which men stand in Christ and His gospel is deeper and more essential than all national, racial, and personal distinctions, Paul, the Jew, stands eager and willing (if God permits) to preach to those also in Rome, the capital of the whole world. How many of us today are ready to go (not wait for them to come) to the universities or to Washington, D.C., to the senators of our country as well as to the culturally and economically deprived of Chicago's South Side?

But what really is the gospel? What would Paul preach in Rome? Why should he go to such trouble?

THE THEME OF HIS LETTER

1:16-17

Initially, his first response to these questions lies in his statement in verses 16-17, and yet the whole rest of the letter does not exhaust the answers.

In the mention of Rome (v. 15), Paul no doubt is excited as he contemplates the capital and theater of the world where he would ultimately come face-to-face with the mighty power concentrated in that stronghold of heathenism and the multitudes of peoples gathered there from every nation of the Mediterranean world. He responds, "I am not ashamed of the gospel," even though for its sake he had been despitefully treated in other great cities such as Athens, Ephesus, and even in Corinth from which he now writes.

His confidence in spite of these hindrances lies in the true greatness of the reality discovered in the message he proclaims. *First* of all, the gospel itself is nothing less than the power of God. This expression "power [Gk. *dynamis*] of God" should not be overlooked. In Paul's usage the power of God is often associated with the wisdom of God in contrast to man's wisdom (1 Cor. 1:24; 2:4; 2 Cor. 6:7). It is a resurrection life power (2 Cor. 13:4), always associated with God's action toward us in Jesus Christ resulting in salvation (1 Cor. 1:18) and actually manifested in some manner in contrast to mere words or ideas (1 Cor. 2:4). Beyond this, how can the decisive activity of God in the human life be analyzed? For Paul no other expression could convey the reality of his own experience and that of others. In the gospel resided the living revelation of God Himself flowing forth to save men.

"Salvation" (Gk. *soteria*) probably conveys the thought of the widest possible inclusion of all God's benefits in Christ to believers. Although not a frequent word of Paul, it certainly is central to his thoughts.[11] In this epistle alone, salvation includes forgiveness of sin and acceptance before God (chaps. 1-4), as well as deliverance from the future wrath of God (5:9), the present new life in the Spirit of God (chaps. 6-8), and the future resurrection of the body (8:11).

Elsewhere in the New Testament Peter teaches that the salvation from sin and darkness to peace and fellowship with God that began in the ministry, death, and resurrection of Jesus will be completed in the future in those who believe. That future salvation is now presently at work in Christians through the power of the gospel (1 Pet. 1:3-5). To this Paul also agrees (Rom. 13:11).

The divine power in the gospel is not dependent upon any human wisdom or virtue or condition such as works done in obedience to any law or ceremony, however sacred. Paul declares that the saving power of God is effective alone by faith "to every one who believes." Faith can only be that response to the gospel of God's saving power that is characterized by obedient trust in the God who has decisively acted in Jesus Christ's death and resurrection to provide for us what we could never do for ourselves (v. 5). It is this attitude of turning away from all self-effort and human devices and casting ourselves totally upon the God and Father of Jesus Christ that effects the mighty working of God's power resulting in our salvation. Salvation is something freely given rather than earned. God gives this grace without regard to merit or national origin, without regard even to special religous distinction. Why, then, "to the Jew first"? Historically the Jews were the first to hear from Jesus' own lips this new thing God would do through Him (Heb. 2:3), and second, because unto them were committed the covenants (Acts 3:26; Rom. 3:2; 9:4).

Second, Paul's confidence is also related to the substance

11. The noun occurs only eighteen times in Paul's letters, including five times in Romans (1:16; 10:1, 10; 11:11; 13:11). The verb form "to save" occurs more frequently (twenty-nine times) including eight times in Romans (5:9, 10; 8:24; 9:27; 10:9, 13; 11:14, 26).

of the gospel, which is spelled out more fully in verse 17. It consists in the manifestation of "the righteousness of God." It might be helpful to show the parallelism between verse 16 and verse 17 in the following manner:

Verse 16	Verse 17
gospel	in it (gospel)
power . . . for salvation	righteousness (life and salvation)
of God	of God
everyone who believes	faith to faith . . . the righteous man shall live by faith

In the gospel the "righteousness [*dikaiosune*] of God" finds expression. But what is the righteousness of God? By the righteousness of God Paul might have meant that quality or attribute of God whereby He reveals Himself to be right or righteous and man sinful. But this could hardly be "good news." Or it could mean the righteousness that God requires of me. But again, how is this good news to me?

In our day, two chief interpretations are advanced based on whether the expression "the righteousness of God" means "God's (own) righteousness" or "a righteousness from God" (NIV). Or, to state it differently, does "righteousness" here mean the saving activity of God or a gift and status conferred on man?

Luther argued that the righteousness of God is that righteousness given to us by God by which we are made righteous (justified). In the Old Testament the righteousness of God can be seen almost as a synonym for salvation in the same way Paul parallels the two in verses 16 and 17 (see also Isa. 46:13; 51:5; Ps. 24:5; 31:1; 98:1, 2; 143:11). So in this view the righteousness of God is that righteousness that He imparts or gives in order to make men righteous (Augustine).[12]

12. For a full discussion of this point and how Paul's concept of justification should be related to the Hebrew concept of righteousness rather than (as usually) the Greek concept, see Norman M. Snaith, *The Distinctive Ideas of the Old Testament* (New York: Schocken, 1964), chaps. 4 and 8 especially.

On the other hand, others argue that the term "the right-eousness of God" means "God's righteousness" and should not be confused with the similar expressions "righteousness" (4:2, 13) or "righteousness from [ex] God" (Phil. 3:9). God's righteousness is His own covenant faithfulness and trust-worthiness whereby He fulfills His promise to Abraham to bring salvation to all people (Gen. 12:3; Gal. 3:7-8). It refers to God's activity in Christ by which He fulfills His covenant promises, effects the satisfaction of His own holiness in the death and resurrection of Jesus for man's sins (3:25-26), and extends to us guilty sinners a free, full pardon and restoration to Himself (justification). Although it is difficult to decide between these two views, the commentary will follow the lat-ter view, at the same time recognizing there are also good reasons to adopt the former.[13]

God's righteousness is revealed "from faith to faith" (v. 17). Though a difficult expression with many interpreta-tions, it seems best to relate this to the parallel in verse 16, "every one who believes," and to understand the phrase to emphasize that salvation (God's righteousness) is solely (ut-terly) by faith.[14] Paul's quotation of Habakkuk 2:4 stresses that the Old Testament taught that this salvation came (sole-

---

13. An unusual amount of attention has been focused recently on this prob-lem. Cranfield and Käsemann favor the first view (see Cranfield, 1:92-99; Ernst Käsemann, *Commentary on Romans* [Grand Rapids: Eerdmans, 1980], pp. 24-30). Sam K. Williams argues convincingly for the second in "The 'Righteousness of God' in Romans," JBL 99 (1980): 241-90; also see J. P. Sanders, *Paul and Palestinian Judaism* (Philadelphia: Fortress, 1977), pp. 491-92.
14. Grammatical parallels to this construction seem to have this effect, e.g., Rom. 6:19, "Lawlessness, resulting in further lawlessness" (utter law-lessness); 2 Cor. 2:16, "death to death" (utter death); Käsemann calls it Semitic rhetoric."

ly) by faith, and the man who has it (the just) also lives by faith (Gal. 3:11; Heb. 10:38).[15]

These two verses contain a rich sampling of Paul's chief words: *gospel, power of God, salvation, faith, Jew, Gentile,* and *righteousness of God.* They have each been touched on briefly in this section, but it will be necessary to return again and again to them in this book as Paul does in his. The scope of the gospel is universal. It is God's saving power for all persons at all times. At the same time the gospel shows forth and interprets God's righteousness. It is this theme that Paul develops in Romans. God's righteousness is experienced by those who will respond to the gospel in obedient trust in Jesus Christ.

* * * * * *

In the following lengthy section (1:18—11:36), Paul argues out the main kernel of his gospel. He first asserts that all—regardless of race, nationality, personal distinctions, or religious heritage—are under God's judgment and stand morally guilty before the Judge of the universe (1:18—3:20). Paul then turns to the provision of the gift of salvation in the sacrificial death of Jesus, the manner in which this provision is secured by faith, and the resulting new life with its abundance (3:21—5:21). He then proceeds to answer two major questions raised by his gospel: What is the relationship be-

---

15. The NIV and NASB ("The righteous man shall live by faith") emphasizes that the just man *lives by faith,* whereas the RSV rendering ("He who through faith is righteous shall live") emphasizes that the person who *by faith is righteous* will live (both now and in the future kingdom). The former sense seems to be the meaning of the Habakkuk passage in the Hebrew, the Targum (Aramaic translation), the LXX, as well as the Qumran commentary on Habakkuk (IQpH8:1-3), Gal. 3:11, and Heb. 10:38 (supported by John Murray, *The Epistle to the Romans* [1:33] following J. B. Lightfoot). Most modern commentators, however, follow the latter sense (RSV), arguing that the immediate context and the structure of the epistle require this emphasis (supported by Nygren, Cranfield (1:102), Käsemann, and Barrett).

tween God's grace and man's freedom? (6:1—8:39); and, What about God's faithfulness in light of the Jews' unbelief? (9:1—11:36).

2

MANKIND'S CONDITION: UNDER THE JUDGMENT OF GOD

1:18—3:20

Paul cannot adequately declare the significance of the manifestation of the righteousness of God (3:21-22) until he has first painted the canvas with the actual human situation in God's sight. Over against God's righteousness stands the unrighteousness of man (1:18-32), as well as the righteousness of man's own making (2:1—3:8). Paul's burden is to show that all men have true moral guilt in the presence of a holy God. Paul will first charge that the Gentiles, or persons who do not have God's written Word, are without excuse before a revealed Creator to whom they are responsible (1:18-32). Second, he turns toward the other major segment of humanity, those who have the written law of God, and accuses them of not keeping this law (2:1—3:8). He finds that both groups, in effect all people, are equally under God's judgment and without hope in themselves (3:9-20).

MAN WITHOUT THE KNOWLEDGE OF THE BIBLE

1:18-32

In only three places in the New Testament do we find material relating to how the gospel was preached to strictly non-Bible-oriented audiences. The first was in Lystra (Acts 14:15-17), where Paul preached to the pagan (though cultured) Lycaonians, but the message is brief and interrupted. Second, in Athens (Acts 17:16-32), Paul again confronts non-Jewish pagan philosophers (Stoics and Epicureans) with the message about Jesus. The third instance comes also from Paul and is found in Romans 1:18-32 and portions of chapter 2. Our generation has rightfully been characterized as the post-Christian age.[1] Out of many past years of biblical emphasis and knowledge, our present western culture reflects the beginning of the emergence of a society largely made up of men without knowledge of the Bible. While some, holding to a nonrational optimism, have entitled our days as the "Age of Aquarius," others more realistically describe our condition as "The Twilight of Western Thought."[2] The fact alone makes the content and approach of this section (1:18-32, 2:1-16) of great importance in understanding how to relate the gospel to our generation.

REVELATION OF GOD'S WRATH (1:18)

Having just spoken of the revelation of God's righteousness (v. 17), Paul turns to the revelation of God's wrath (v. 18). Someone might say, "Why do I need salvation?" Paul answers: "Because you are under the wrath of God." "But why am I under His wrath?" "Because you suppress the truth."

Before commenting on these questions and answers, it might be helpful to clear up the problem of the relationship between this section (v. 18) and the previous (vv. 16-17). Some see Paul taking a long digression that continues until he resumes the thought about the gospel in 3:21. This is a mis-

1. Dorothy L. Sayers, *Christian Letters to a Post-Christian World* (Grand Rapids: Eerdmans, 1969); Francis A. Schaeffer, *The God Who Is There* (Downers Grove, Ill.: Inter-Varsity, 1968); *Escape from Reason* (Downers Grove, Ill.: Inter-Varsity, 1968); *Death in the City* (Downers Grove, Ill.: Inter-Varsity, 1969); and Os Guiness, *The Dust of Death* (Downers Grove, Ill.: Inter-Varsity, 1972). This expression is of course relative. The present situation could be reversed at any time by a worldwide revival.

2. See book of similar title by the Dutch philosopher Hermann Dooyeweerd, *In the Twilight of Western Thought* (Philadelphia: Presb. & Ref., 1960); see especially Donald Bloesch, *The Crumbling of the Foundations* (Grand Rapids: Zondervan, 1984).

take for two reasons. First, it ignores the ordinary sense of the Greek particle "for" (*gar*) that begins verse 18 and intimately binds the thought of this verse to verse 17. Second, the word "revealed" (and tense) Paul uses for the wrath of God (v. 18) is identical to the word (and tense) he uses in reference to the righteousness of God (v. 17). Even though the thought is complicated, it seems to run along these lines: just as the future salvation of believers is now in the present being revealed in the gospel of Jesus Christ and appropriated by faith, so both the past wrath of God against sin (as demonstrated in Calvary's events) as well as the future wrath of God (2:5) is now in the present revealed both in the preaching of the gospel and in the human scene and experienced by those who turn away from the truth of God.

Whatever else, it seems clear from this connection that the true preaching of the gospel can only occur with the concurrent preaching of the real wrath of God upon men. This truth is lacking among many of our generation of gospel preachers.[3] Wrath is God's dynamic and personal (though never malicious) reaction against sin (3:5; 9:22), and it has cosmic significance in that it is "from heaven."

But why is God's wrath directed toward me? Because I in my "ungodliness and unrighteousness" suppress the truth.[4]

---

3. "There is no real preaching of the Christian gospel except in light of the fact that man is under the wrath of God" (Schaeffer, *Death in the City,* p. 93). It also seems evident that the true wrath of God is only seen against the background of the norm in the gospel—the righteousness of God in Jesus Christ. Cranfield remarks: "It is that we do not see the full meaning of the wrath of God in the disasters befalling sinful man in the course of history: the reality of the wrath of God is only truly known when it is seen in its revelation in Gethsemane and on Golgotha" (*A Critical and Exegetical Commentary on the Epistle to the Romans,* 1:110).

4. The terms "ungodliness" and "unrighteousness" are best understood as an emphatic expression of one and the same thing (Anders Nygren, *Commentary on Romans* [Philadelphia: Fortress, 1949], p. 101). The single expression "in unrighteousness" of the latter phrase seems to confirm this. Man's moral condition of unrighteousness is never separated from religious corruption and is seen by Paul as a result of man's religious apostasy.

Paul's word for "suppress" ("hold" in the KJV) is important but unfortunately ambiguous in the Greek (*katechō*). It may mean, and often does, to "hold to" something such as spiritual values (1 Thess. 5:21). In this case Paul would be saying that in spite of our unrighteousness we still "hold to" a certain basic truth about our existence.[5] On the other hand, because he is developing the thought of our refusal to acknowledge the truth of God implicit in the creation (vv. 19-20), we prefer the alternate idea in the word. We "hold back" or "resist" (Luke 4:42; 2 Thess. 2:6-7) the truth of God as Creator so that truth does not find expression in our lives (v. 21).[6]

REVELATION OF THE KNOWLEDGE OF GOD (1:19-20)

But how can God direct His wrath toward me for suppressing the truth of His Creatorship when I have never even heard of the God of the Bible or the gospel? The answer is that all men know certain truths about God (v. 19). How? "For" (reason number 1) God has continually in past history, as long as there has been a universe, (and in the present) revealed Himself among men through the created order of existence. This knowledge of God, though limited, is nevertheless real and clear ("clearly seen"), even though men's suppression of it has to them dimmed or extinguished it.

Calvin's remark is striking: "In saying that *God manifested it,* he means that the purpose for which man is created is to be the spectator of the fabric of the world; the purpose for which eyes have been given him is that by gazing on so fair an image he may be led on to its Author."[7] What is manifested to them and thus known to all men everywhere is God's "eternal power and divine nature" (v. 20)—that is, that God is God

---

5. Schaeffer, *Death in the City,* p. 102, explains Paul's thought thus: "They . . . hold some of the truth about themselves and about the universe . . . but they refuse to carry these truths to their reasonable conclusions."
6. Perhaps even "to hold imprisoned" (TDNT, 2:829).
7. John Calvin, *Epistle of Paul to the Romans,* trans. Ross MacKensie (Grand Rapids: Eerdmans, 1961), p. 31.

and not man. Man perceives in the created existence not only his own finiteness, but because of God's revelation to him he knows his creatureliness. He knows that he is not the autonomous (independent) center of his life and world, but that God as Creator and Lord stands infinitely above him as the Source and Goal of his created life.[8] Therefore Paul can say of all of us: "So that they are without excuse."[9]

I, then, may be justly visited with the wrath of God because, though I may not have heard about God in the Bible or in the gospel, I have suppressed this rudimentary truth of my creatureliness that God continually makes available to me in (or, by) "what has been made."[10] God does not reap (wrath) where He has not sown (knowledge).

REJECTION OF THE KNOWLEDGE OF GOD (1:21-23)

In these verses (21-23) Paul gives a second reason ("for" in v. 21) God justly visits His wrath on us. Not only do we have the possibility of knowing God through creation and history and fail to do so; Paul indicates the root of the matter is that we actually possessed a knowledge of God ("knew God"), but failed in a proper acknowledgement: "They did not honor Him as God, or give thanks [to Him]" (v. 21). Instead we became senseless and practiced disobedience (idolatry) and rebellion. Our failure was not so much that we failed to recognize God, but that we would not acknowledge God as *Lord* and live in grateful obedience—in fact (in Paul's view),

---

8. These verses do not argue for the Thomistic natural theology or natural religion. Paul does not have in mind deductive (Aristotelian) logical arguments that can prove God's existence, but as vv. 21-23 show, he is referring to an actual continuous revelation of God to all men that they possess (which could not be true of logical systems leading to belief in God) but have abandoned. The traditional logical arguments for God's existence do not prove God exists but simply show that once God is assumed, then the world can be logically and adequately explained.
9. The "so that" indicates not merely result but purpose.
10. Or "in His works." Not only in the beginning but throughout the whole history of mankind, God has made Himself known in His works (Nygren, p. 104). Cranfield, however, prefers the traditional sense of 'things made' rather than works in general (1:115).

to "believe" is to have "faith." Rather, we chose to be our own Lord ("professing themselves to be wise"). By throwing off our obligations to God, we thought to rise above creatureliness. Instead the new gods of our own making, which we exchanged for the Creator, while for a time our servants, eventually became our masters and brought us to a more debased and lower state than before. In the end we "worshipped and served the creature" (vv. 23, 25).

Five steps downward have been noted in this whole process, beginning significantly with the attitude of the heart of rebellion against lordship, in that we honored Him not, neither were we thankful, but rather futile in our speculations, and professing to be wise, we exchanged the glory of God (vv. 21-23): (1) practical indifference to God's truth, (2) worthless speculation about God, (3) death of the God idea, (4) pride of human reason, and (5) fetishism (devotion to occult objects). This whole description should be understood as a sort of philosophy of heathenism's development in any given setting and not as an historical account of a specific religious apostasy.

Here it may be appropriate to ask a few questions about pagan religions (nontheistic) and idolatry. It has been popular since the resurgence in recent days of comparative religious studies to think of the world religions as preparatory to Christianity. In them, we are told, God is revealed to man in an incomplete fashion, whereas in Christianity the full revelation of God is seen. But Paul saw no divine revelation in all the heathen religions. It is not God who is revealed in the non-Christian religions of the world but rather the corruption of man; not God's truth but man's falsehood.[11] While there is a general revelation of God given in all the world, this revelation is generally suppressed and opposed by sinful man. Actually the pagan religions of the world, which display a good bit of commonality, find their commonality not in some true knowledge of God but in a common reaction to the revelation

11. Nygren, p. 108.

of God that comes to them continually in the things that are made. Nonbiblical religions are a reaction, an answer, a resistance to, and a defense against God's revelation. Disobedience, not obedience, is the explanation of the commonality. However, this fact does not exclude the possibility that some individuals within these systems may have responded to this true revelation of God (2:14-15). So the very presence of false religion in the world is evidence of the continual revelation of God that leaves all men inexcusably guilty before Him.[12] Nevertheless, the Christian attitude toward those who follow different religions should never be one of superiority. D. T. Niles beautifully captured the true relationship of the Christian to others of different faiths by stating that we come to them as "one beggar telling another beggar where he found bread."

Is there idolatry in the Western world today? Idolatry begins in the mind when we pervert our idea of God into something other than what He really is.[13] Luther said, "Whatever your heart clings to and relies on is your god." Science, reason, progress, secularism, pleasure, nationalism, militarism, and mysticism have become for many the new gods of the Western world.[14] To us today comes the gospel with its call to radical conversion in the midst of the modern pantheon of gods.

12. See G. C. Berkouwer, *General Revelation* (Grand Rapids: Eerdmans, 1952), chap. 7, "Revelation and Knowledge," for a full discussion of this thesis; also Dooyeweerd, "What is Man?" *In the Twilight of Western Thought;* William M. Ramsay, "The Pauline Philosophy of History," in *The Cities of St. Paul* (Grand Rapids: Baker, 1960).
13. A. W. Tozer, *The Knowledge of the Holy* (New York: Harper & Row, 1961), p. 11.
14. Note also the rapid increase today of occultism, oriental mysticism, and drugs, which may be a transitional stage on the road to a full-blown reversion to idolatry. See Jacques Ellul, *The New Demons* (New York: Seabury, 1975); Bloesch, *The Crumbling of the Foundations;* and the non-Christian Naomi R. Goldenberg, *Changing of the Gods: Feminism and the End of Traditional Religions* (Boston: Beacon, 1979).

RESULTS OF THE REJECTION OF THE KNOWLEDGE OF GOD (1:24-32)

In these final verses of the chapter, Paul shows how the wrath of God works its way out in the concrete human situation of men who have abandoned God as Lord. Let it be repeated that this does not mean there will be no final wrath of God in all the future (2:5), but even now in history God makes His wrath operative. Paul indicates this by three times repeating the same dire expression, "God gave them over" (vv. 24, 26, 28). Not that God makes men sin, but He abandons them to their own passions as a form of His wrath. This is an awesome truth. In modern societies moral permissiveness, especially in its sexual perversion and inversion, can be seen as God's acts of wrath upon those who have turned away from the truth and have suppressed the acknowledgement of God as God. The point is that man is really a significant being in a significant history. When he chooses to abandon God and make himself lord, he is abandoned by God to his own lusts. Since man is not only an individual but a social creature, when he chooses to leave God, he also affects his fellow men in society as well as his descendants.

Today's culture everywhere reflects the loneliness, despair, fragmentation, and loss of personal identity that results from the sense in man of the loss of God. To many, God is dead, but so is man.[15] Our culture is increasingly characterized by relativism, which teaches that all values are personal, shifting opinions; there is no objective truth or right. Nowhere has the tendency to try to relativize absolutes become more evident than in the erosion of conscience in the moral realm.[16] One characteristic of our day is nihilism, the determined effort to

15. Some materials on this are the books of Francis A. Schaeffer already cited; Kenneth Hamilton, *In Search of Contemporary Man* (Grand Rapids: Eerdmans, 1967); C. Stephen Evans, *Despair: A Moment or a Way of Life?* (Downers Grove, Ill.: Inter-Varsity, 1971); John W. Sanderson, Jr., *Encounter in the Non-Christian Era* (Grand Rapids: Zondervan, 1970); Bloesch, *The Crumbling of the Foundations*.
16. By "moral realm" we mean the whole spectrum of human values including, but not limited to, sexual values.

destroy everything, to break down every institution, every system of thought, every abiding norm. Nihilism begins with the abandonment of God. Without God there are no abiding truths, lasting principles, or norms, and man is cast upon a sea of speculation and skepticism and attempted self-salvation.

So Paul continues with, "God gave them over in the lusts of their hearts to impurity, that their bodies might be dishonored among them" (v. 24). In their freedom from God's absolutes they turned to perversion and even inversion of the created order. In the end their humanism (man-centeredness) resulted in dehumanization of each other. To "dishonor" their bodies must refer not to the normal sexual relations of married couples (which in the Bible is always beautiful), but, as Paul will show (vv. 26-27), to perverted sex and inverted relations of homosexual acts. This fate came to those who "exchanged the truth of God [see v. 21] for a [Gk. "the"] lie [that *man* is absolute]" (v. 25).

Because men and women inverted the creature-Creator relationship, God visits them with the hideous results of creature-creature inversion. In the rest of the chapter nothing new is added to this point until verse 32, but a number of illustrations are given of how God's abandonment of men and women to their own desires works in the personal and social realms.

In verse 26 Paul again repeats the pathetic sounding, "God gave them over," that connects the moral degradation to their apostasy from God, and goes on to speak first of the perversion of the created order (natural) by women. While male homosexual acts are clearly in Paul's mind in verse 27, some feel that the female counterpart (lesbianism) is not expressly described in verse 26. Yet the "in the same way" of verse 27 seems to indicate that he is describing in verse 26 the same kind of sin in the female as he goes on to condemn in males.

Homosexual activity (v. 27) among males is further evidence of the inversion of the created order ("abandoned the natural function of the woman"), which results in "indecent acts." They are now receiving that "due penalty of their error" (of worshiping the creation, v. 25). What due penalty? Perhaps Paul refers to the gnawing unsatisfied lust itself, together with the dreadful physical and moral consequnces of debauchery. This sin, it must be borne in mind, is not worse than other sins or one that removes us from the human race or the grace of God. Those caught up in homosexual sins need compassion like any other sinner, but it must be pointed out that homosexual activity is wrong, and the increase of this practice in today's society (as in Paul's) is further evidence of mankind's apostasy from the truth of God.[17]

Paul adds in verse 28 the reason for this debauchery: "Just as they did not see fit to acknowledge God any longer, God gave them over to a depraved mind." Something of the Greek play on words is lost in the English. It goes like this: "As they found God worthless to their knowledge . . . God gave them over to a worthless [depraved] mind." Having first chosen in their unrighteousness to suppress God's truth as it was revealed to them, men were given over by God to a form of thinking that practices "things which are not proper" or things not fitting in God's moral order (obscenities). How we live quite often determines how we think. When we live a while in a particular sinful manner, our minds begin to justify and rationalize our actions.

There follows in verses 29-31 a listing of various sins that illustrate Paul's point. They almost defy classification or groupings. Among them are personal sins, social sins, sins of pride, greed, injustice, perversions. It is a picture of utmost degeneracy. A meditation on these shows at once how complete a disorientation of the life results when the creature is alienated from the Creature.

There is a species of ant that lives in some parts of Africa: it lives in subterranean tunnels many feet in the earth, where the

---

17. Current estimates number homosexuals (male and female, exclusive or substantive) in the United States at about 20 million or between 6 to 10 percent of the population (*The American Psychological Monitor,* 1974). Figures over the last ten years have not varied significantly.

young are sheltered and the queen is housed. The workers go on foraging trips to distant places, returning to the nest with that on which the colony feeds. It is said that if, while they are away, their queen is molested, the workers, far away, become nervous and uncoordinated. If she is killed, they become frantic, rush around aimlessly, and eventually die in the field. It is thought that the workers in the normal situation are constantly oriented to the queen by some radarlike device; if she is killed, all orientation ceases, and frenzy ensues, a frenzy that ends in death. Can we find a better parable of man in his alienation?

Paul concludes in verse 32 with, "Although they know the ordinance [sentence] of God, that those who practice such things are worthy of [eternal] death, they not only do the same [occasionally, in a more restricted way], but also give hearty approval [Gk. *syneudokeō,* "agree with" or "applaud"] to those who practice [habitually] them."[18] To do these things against one's sense of right is culpable, but to be in moral agreement with others who practice these obscenities (even if one does not do them) shows that the sympathies lie there and renders those persons inexcusable. That those who are without the Bible "know the ordinance of God" seems to anticipate the argument from conscience in 2:14-15.

In summation of Paul's argument dealing with those without the knowledge of the Bible (1:18-32), it may be said that (1) the visible revelation of God's wrath upon the pagan world can be seen most clearly in their moral perversions and

18. The Greek word here translated "practice" is *prassō,* meaning "habitually practice." It is much stronger than the word "commit" (KJV). "Those who condone and applaud the vicious actions of others are actually making a deliberate contribution to the setting up of a public opinion favorable to vice, and so to the corruption of an indefinite number of other people. So, for example, to excuse or gloss over the use of torture by security forces or the cruel injustices of racial discrimination and oppression, while not being involved in them directly, is to help to cloak monstrous evil with an appearance of respectability and so to contribute most effectively to its firmer entrenchment" (Cranfield, 1:135).

inversions (individual and social) of the created order; (2) these perversions are the direct result of their exchanging the worship of the Creator for the creation; and (3) they are under the judgment of God and inexcusable because God has made the rudimentary knowledge of Himself continuously available to all men, yet this knowledge has been willfully suppressed.

So, why do those without the Bible's knowledge need the salvation offered in the gospel? Because they are under the wrath (judgment) of God. Why are they under the wrath of God? Because they have individually suppressed God's Lordship in their lives, and they have inherited a perverted religious tradition.

What evidence is there from the human situation that God's wrath is already being manifested? Paul finds the proof in the moral degradation of societies and of the lives of those who have been abandoned to follow their whimsical lusts.

Paul has not yet brought all men under this judgment. He must now consider the case of those who possess the knowledge of God in the Bible.

MAN WITH THE KNOWLEDGE OF THE BIBLE

2:1—3:8

Although Paul no doubt has both the proud Jew and the proud cultured Gentile (Greek and Roman) in mind in 2:1-16, he does not specifically mention the Jew until verse 17. His burden consists in showing that those who have not sunk to the depths of depravity that some in the pagan world have, because they have the light of God's will in the Bible, are nevertheless under the same judgment of God. Not the possession of the knowledge of the truth but the practice of the spirit of the truth shows who has really acknowledged the Creator. The idea that God shows no partiality (2:11) means that the proud Jew is brought to judgment on the same basis as the Gentile, as Paul will illustrate in more detail (vv. 12-16).

Turning directly to the Jews in verse 17, he accuses them of false pride in both their religious knowledge (vv. 17-25) and in their religious rite of circumcision (vv. 25-29). Finally, Paul discusses the main advantages of being a Jew (3:1-4) and answers objections to his position (3:5-8).

PRINCIPLE OF GOD'S JUDGMENT: NO PARTIALITY (2:1-11)

After having just heard the detailed description of the plight of the pagan world, a morally minded person might heartily agree with Paul's condemnation and even at this point offer an amen. But how can "good" people who are not idolators come under Paul's sweeping thesis that all have sinned and that they can only be delivered by the righteousness of God in the gospel?

In our day there are many moralistic people in and out of the churches. We generally think of them as middle- or upper middle-class society, the "moral majority." Many of these people still attempt in principle to hold to the basic Christian morality but have abandoned the radical biblical religious root of regeneration. They want the fruit of Christianity without its root, personal relationship to Jesus Christ. What of these, Paul? His answer consists of charging that the critic of others has condemned himself, because the criticism of such sinners (1:18-32) reveals that in the act of criticism he knows what is right and has no excuse for his own violation of God's law (vv. 1-3).

In verse 1, Paul strikes an immediate blow to the conscience of the moralist by asserting, "Therefore [because what was true of those in 1:18-32] is also true of the self-righteous critic] you are without excuse [see also 1:20 for the same word!], every man of you [whether Jew or pagan moralist], who passes judgment . . . you condemn yourself." "Every man of you" (or "my good man") alerts us that Paul has in mind here (and throughout the letter) a real objecter or heckler.[19]

The moralist might say, "The wrath of God justly rests on the debauched, idolatrous Gentiles but not on the Jews." There are two reasons why the moralist is on thin ice with respect to the judgment of God. In the first place, he reveals by his criticism of the heathen vices that he knows God's moral requirement. He cannot plead ignorance of God's will. And yet Paul alleges they "practice the same things." Not that these people were necessarily homosexuals or violent or disobedient to parents, but they were sinners (vv. 21-24, stealing, adultery, sacrilege) and broke the same law of God that the pagans violated in grosser fashion. E. J. Carnell has noted, "Self-righteous people make one of two capital mistakes: either they misunderstand the height of God's law or they misunderstand the depth of their own moral conduct."[20]

Second, behind all the sins in 1:29-32 lies the sin of idolatry, which reveals man's ambition to put himself in the place of God and so be his own Lord.[21] But is this not precisely what the judge does when he assumes the right to condemn his own fellow creatures and excuse himself (James 4:11-12)? True, God's judgment rightly falls on the pagan (v. 2), but do you think *you* of all men, *you* who know God's will can do as they do and yet get away with it ("escape," v. 3)? Anticipating his answer, Paul would say no, "for there is no partiality with God" (v. 11).

Furthermore, since the moralist has escaped the present

19. This diatribe style was common to the philosophers and preachers in Paul's day. It is not impossible that some of the arguments in this book were first worked out by Paul in actual confrontation and debate with non-Christians as they interjected remarks and received Paul's replies (3:5-8; 6:1, 15).
20. E. J. Carnell, *Christian Commitment* (Grand Rapids: Eerdmans, 1957), p. 202.
21. C. K. Barrett, *The Epistle to the Romans,* p. 44.

wrath of God to a large extent because he has not so overtly suppressed the truth as has the man without the Bible, he should not misread God's kindness to him (in not immediately visiting wrath) as if such delay were an indication that God has somehow favored him. The moralist should repent of his sin and wickedness and realize that God judges on the basis of a man's work or deeds and not on the basis of his national or religious heritage (vv. 4-11).

These verses (4-11) touch on the vital matter of the future judgment of God. Is there a literal future hell?[22] Paul, it seems, speaks unhesitatingly in verse 5 of "the day of wrath and revelation of the righteous judgment of God." The moralist wrongly thinks that he will escape God's judgment by taking God's side and condemning the unrighteous person (vv. 1-3). Further, he is also in error in thinking that because of his religious and national heritage he is excused from judgment, and God is now extending special favor ("kindness, forbearance and patience," v. 4) to him.[23]

But all such thinking is wrong, because God's judgment is completely impartial (v. 11). He judges not on the basis of who the person is, but with respect alone to the nature of the deeds he has done (v. 6). The religious moralist (Jew or pagan) must recognize that God's kindness (absence of visible judgment) is extended to him out of grace. Rather than interpret this "forbearance" (Gk. *anochē,* restraint) as a special favor in judgment, God's longsuffering should be viewed as a persuasive force to try to bring men to their knees in "repentance" and faith (v. 4).

The Jew of Paul's day thought that, because he was receiv-

22. If 1:18-32 gives us some indication of the present result of the wrath of God in the loss of man's humanity, then the future withdrawal of all (perhaps not *all;* even in judgment there is mercy) of God's grace and kindness from man can only be dreadfully imagined. "Deprivation," rather than the medieval imagery of burning or physical pain (e.g. Dante's *Inferno*), may depict more of the biblical concept (see C. S. Lewis, *Problem of Pain* [New York: Macmillan, 1961], pp. 106-16).
23. These ideas can be seen in the Jewish Apocryphal book of the *Wisdom of Solomon* (15:1-4), which Paul evidently knew.

ing little wrath now from God, it must be evidence that in the future life he would have unmixed reward. In reality, Paul declares, they were by their "unrepentant heart . . . storing up wrath" (v. 5)[24] against themselves for the future day of judgment. This unexpected inversion by Paul clearly reminds us that a form of supposed sincerity, even before God, can be sincerely misleading because of man's sinfulness and may lead to eternal judgment.

Verses 7-9 have been a source of perplexity to many Christians. In them Paul establishes the truth that God's judgment of all men will be on the basis of their works or deeds. This thought has led many Protestants to feel an uncomfortable tension over what appears to be a contradiction between salvation by faith alone, without works, and Paul's teaching here. In brief, the solution (as well as the tension) lies in understanding the nature of the works to which Paul here makes mention.

First, Paul considers those described as receiving "eternal life" (v. 7). Most of the translations have missed the actual thought of Paul. Paraphrased, the Greek would mean something like this: "To those who with patient endurance in good work (as an outward life-style) seek for the glory, honor, and incorruption God alone can give (as the object of their inward motivation), He will render eternal life." Those who by their good works prove they seek the things that alone are God's are contrasted in verse 8 with those who are self-seekers, who

24. The Greek tense (connotative present) can signify action being attempted but not successfully completed (e.g., John 13:6); in such cases "tries to" supplies a good auxiliary (F. Blass and A. Debrunner, *A Greek Grammar of the New Testament and Other Early Christian Literature,* ed. and trans. Robert W. Funk [Chicago: U. of Chicago, 1961], par. 319, p. 167). Repentance (Greek, *metanoia*) in the New Testament does not basically signify sorrow for sin or even remorse, but stands for the radical change in thought and will that turns a person away from himself to acknowledge God as Lord, and away from disobedience of God's will to obedience. For Paul, repentance is divinely worked (2 Cor. 7:9-11) and includes the action of faith in Jesus Christ (the latter is Paul's more common word).

are "selfishly ambitious and do not obey the truth."[25] The self-seeker suppresses the truth in unrighteousness (v. 8); and against such the wrath and fury of God are directed (1:18).

The "doing good" in verse 7 (contrast, "does evil," v. 9) refers to the whole Christian life of righteousness through faith in Christ that Paul will develop later. The patient continuance in good works (Eph. 2:10) demonstrates that the life's source is faith in God and the gospel. The real issue is whether a man sees his good works as evidence that he is doing a good job for God, or whether (as in Paul's view) he sees them as marks not of human achievement but of hope in God.

There can be no question, then, of God's showing any special favoritism (Matt. 5:45). Each man faces an impartial Judge who will determine whether the life was lived in pursuit of God's glory or in self-seeking unrighteousness (v. 11).

GOD'S JUDGMENT AND THE KNOWLEDGE OF THE LAW (2:12-16)

"But Paul," one might interject, "you forget that the Jew has had the privilege of God's special revelation in the Bible (law). Doesn't this give him an advantage over the heathen whom God has not so blessed?" In verses 12-16 Paul begins to break down yet another prop. The sorest point of all for the Jew was Paul's contention that there is no protection from the wrath of God in the possession of the Bible (law): "For not the hearers [listeners—Sabbath by Sabbath] of the Law are just before God, but the doers of the Law will be justified" (v. 13).[26] It is performance of God's will, not possession (or knowledge) that averts the wrath of God (James 1:22). God's revelation (law) does not protect one

25. Greek for "selfishly ambitious" is *eritheia,* which is derived from a word meaning "hireling." The idea, then, is not "contentious" (KJV) but "base self-seeking" since they use their works as evidence of human achievement (see TDNT, 2:660); also Cranfield, 1:148.
26. Hypothetically at least, this seems to be the point. In Gal. 3:21 Paul argues that, if a law could have given life, then surely righteousness would have come to man through the keeping of the Mosaic law, but since all are sinners and transgressors of the intent of the law, God brought righteousness to man in a different manner.

from judgment. It is rather the instrument for a more severe reckoning with the exceeding sinfulness of sin (7:7). More knowledge brings more responsibility and greater accountability. Thus the law becomes the possessor's accuser—his destruction, not his salvation.

In order to maintain his thesis of the equality before God of both those without and those with the Bible, Paul must answer yet another objection. "If the law will be my standard of judgment," the religious moralist might object, "how can God treat the pagan equally with me when he has no law to judge him? Won't the absence of the law to judge him allow the pagan to escape God's wrath?" "No," Paul answers, "because though the pagan is without the biblical revelation (law of Moses), he is not thereby outside all revelation from God ('law to themselves,' v. 14)." How does the pagan without the Bible have the knowledge of God's will? More disturbingly, are the heathen lost because they are without the knowledge of the Bible and Christ's gospel? In trying to answer these questions, we must be careful to note what Paul does say on this point and what he does not say.

Some quite convincingly argue that Paul is referring to Christian Gentiles in verse 14 when he says, "When Gentiles who do not have the Law do instinctively the things of the Law. . . ." He would then be anticipating his argument later on about justification without the law for all (3:21-28). An objection to this view might point out that Paul says these Gentiles have no knowledge *at all* of the law, and yet they do "instinctively" what the law requires—both of which characteristics would hardly be true of Gentile Christians. Yet the NASB and NIV translation of this verse is arbitrary, and the phrase in question could be equally well rendered: "When Gentiles who do not have the law by nature (i.e., by birth) do what the law requires. . . ." They are doers of the law, not in the sense that they earn salvation by law-keeping or that they know it fully, but in the sense that their faith in Christ has put them into a positive relation to the law (or will of God) because they now have it in their hearts and desire earnestly to fulfill its moral requirements (v. 15).[27] It is difficult to decide between the two views. The following discussion will develop the alternative, more popular view while recognizing the strength of the Gentiles-as-Christians approach.

It will help to begin with the matter of the "conscience," whose role Paul describes as "bearing witness" (v. 15). Conscience is not acquired through our environment. Rather, man finds himself already in his earliest years functioning morally as a creature made in the image of God. Dogs or other domesticated animals seem to have a conscience only because of their association with man. Conscience is the person functioning in the native act of deciding right from wrong. It is important to note that this small voice within does not function legislatively but only judicially. Conscience assumes the presence of a valid norm. It anticipates a complementary something whereby it may then govern itself. As an umpire, it does not make the rules but decides in the light of the existing rules. It refuses to be normless. That conscience is innate in every human being is unquestioned; what standard it approves or disapproves is quite a different matter. The content, or norm, by which the conscience decides the right from the wrong is not innate, or at least not entirely innate, but is controlled by God's revelation, the creation order, the environment, and local social standards.[28] Conscience, therefore, can be educated or changed by the introduction of new norms.

27. See Cranfield for a thorough articulation of this view through verses 12-16. He cites Augustine and Ambrosiaster as early—and Barth more recently—exponents of the same view (1:156). For the alternate view, see Ernst Käsemann, *Commentary on Romans*, pp. 62-68.

28. This is well-illustrated in the story told by a missionary to northern Brazil. He had observed a very nervous and fidgety native with sweat on his brow enter the village and seem very uneasy even in the presence of his friends. Later, the missionary had learned that this fellow had just killed a man of another tribe. Although in this society it was not considered wrong to kill a member of another tribe, this man was obviously under the pressure of a guilty conscience. While societal norms do set the conscience, there is also the witness of God in the nature of our relations with other human beings that overrides the errant social standard.

Scripture refers to a dulled or calloused conscience. Through repeated ignorings of the "no" voice, the moral faculty grows numb (1 Tim. 4:2). The familiar experience of repeatedly shutting off the alarm clock in the morning and then going back to sleep illustrates in the physical-psychic realm how the conscience in the moral realm can be ignored until we no longer hear its voice. If we convince ourselves in a relativized society that there are no norms, then the function of conscience will deteriortate.

Paul says that there are three witnesses that agree together that the pagan has a basic knowledge of right and wrong (a norm), even though he does not have the written revelation of God. They are: (1) the outward (phenomenological) or natural ("instinctively," v. 14) establishment of societal laws for controlling behavior; (2) the conscience, which judges each man concerning his own actions with reference to the natural norms (v. 15); and (3) alternately accusing or else excusing thoughts we have about the behaviors of others that may be publicly debated (v. 15).[29]

The pagan, by natural moral instinct, sets up certain social standards that include some of the same rules as the laws of God in the Bible, such as the pursuit of lawful vocations, the procreation of offspring, filial and natural affections, the care of the poor and sick, and numerous other natural virtues required by the Mosaic law. Paul teaches that since he does

29. The construction is very difficult in the Greek. Two possibilities exist here grammatically: (1) the idea of "meanwhile . . . one another" (KJV) (Gk. *metaxy allēlōn*) refers to mutual judgment of each other's behavior and is different from, though not unrelated to, the functioning of conscience; or (2) these words refer to their inward thoughts: "their conflicting thoughts accuse or perhaps excuse them" (RSV). It is difficult to decide, though the KJV idea seems better. See H. P. Liddon, *An Explanatory Analysis of St. Paul's Epistle to the Romans* (Grand Rapids: Zondervan, 1961), pp. 46-49; Nygren, p. 125; William Sanday and Arthur Headlam, *A Critical and Exegetical Commentary on the Epistle to the Romans* (Edinburgh: T. & T. Clark, 1900), p. 60. Cranfield again argues that this whole process takes place not in the present but in the future judgment, where Gentile Christians will be reminded both of their failures of complete obedience and of the fact that their thoughts have been changed through faith in Christ toward obedience (1:162).

this, he is not without a law to judge him. The "things of the Law" (v. 14) that the Gentiles do naturally must mean certain things the biblical law also requires. We should not take this to mean that the whole Mosaic law or even all the Ten Commandments are written on the hearts of pagans. Paul does not say this. Similarly, the expression "work of the Law" (v. 15) is not the law itself but the effect of the law, that is, the setting of the conscience. So in effect he himself (in virtue of being a person) becomes a law (norm) to himself.

In other words, there is something, Paul argues, in the very pattern of created human existence that should (and sometimes does) lead the Gentile to an attitude of humble, grateful, dependent creatureliness. There does exist a moral standard among the heathen not identical to, but certainly similar to, certain things in the Bible.[30] This similarity, Paul says, is not simply coincidental but reflects God's revelation of His will to man in conscience and in the natural or created order (1:20-21). When the pagan violates this standard, he stands under the judgment of God and should in humble repentance cast himself upon the mercy of the Creator for forgiveness. His sin consists principally in his failure through rebellion to humble himself—nevertheless God will judge him on the basis of the specific violations of his own conscience.[31] Can he be saved? Paul does not answer this question directly. Our answer will depend on whether we believe (1) that the knowledge of God revealed to the pagan is enough for salvation, and (2) that such people do *de facto* respond positively to this revelation of God. A *no* response to either of these would justify Christian missions.

30. C. S. Lewis states, "There have been differences between their moralities [speaking of different civilizations and ages], but these have never amounted to anything like a total difference" (*Mere Christianity* [New York: Macmillan, 1943], p. 5).
31. It seems that missionary as well as evangelistic effort among young people in our country should pay closer attention to this point. We may see places where another is violating *our* standards, but our point of contact with him may have to be in an area where he is actually rejecting by his life a standard that he has committed himself to. This is an area where he will feel guilty.

So Paul concludes this section by returning in verse 16 to the thought of verse 13. We connect the words from verse 13, "not the hearers of the Law are just before God, but the doers of the Law will be justified" with those in verse 16, "on the day when . . . God will judge the secrets of men." Yet the reference to "the secrets of men" shows that Paul also includes in this summary verse his thoughts expressed in verses 14-15—that not only men's outward deeds, but also their inner motivations, feelings, and thoughts will be the subject matter of God's examination in the future day of judgment. The standards of judgment will be Paul's gospel,[32] that is, the very truths he has been revealing in chapters one and two; and the agent of judgment will be Jesus Christ Himself (John 5:27; Acts 17:31).[33]

THE LAW AND JEWISH PERFORMANCE (2:17-24)

Paul now turns directly to the Jew who has the written law of God. He is still dealing with the thought of God's universal judgment on all men and the further principle that it is not the listeners to the law who are right before God but the doers of the law. Paul has already rejected the fallacy that the Jew has a special privilege and advantage before God even when he does not respond appropriately (2:14-15). Now he wants to nail this down further and leave no way of escape. It was not that the Jew was wrong in prizing his possession of the law and esteeming its knowledge an advantage. The problem was that he trusted in the mere knowledge and possession of the

32. Not Paul's gospel in distinction to Jesus' or Peter's or John's gospel, but the gospel Paul taught as the norm and with which the other apostles were in agreement (see Gal. 2:9).
33. Although the Christian is never described by Paul or any NT writer as being saved by works but ever by faith alone, yet saving faith is never alone. Salvation involves the life we are saved to as well as the life we are saved from. We are saved to holiness and good works (Eph. 2:10). Thus, although judgment always proceeds on the basis of works (Rev. 20:12), God's salvation is never on the basis of works but always faith. Yet the outworking of this salvation produces a life-style characterized by good works before God, and therefore the principle of God's judgment is maintained even in the case of the believer (1 Cor. 3:11-13).

law and clung merely to its outward observances. But a certain kind of Jew in Paul's day did not let the law convict him of his sin and lead him into obedient faith that would result in his keeping the real intent of the law. The moralist thus reveals his rebellion against God, not by his outward immorality and corruption, but by the hardening of his heart (2:5) and by his refusal to repent of his bankrupt self-righteousness.

In verses 17-20 Paul sets forth the acknowledged advantage on which the Jew prided himself: (1) "bear the name 'Jew' " (a member of the covenant people); (2) "rely upon the Law" (trusted the law for his standing before God); (3) "boast in God" (the true worship of God); (4) "know His will" (the revealed will of God); (5) "approve the things that are essential" (keen sense of moral discernment); (6) "guide to the blind" (in spiritual insight and light for them in darkness); (7) "corrector of the foolish" (unlearned); and (8) "a teacher of the immature" (last word in proper parental education). He could do all this confidently because he had the "embodiment of knowledge and of the truth" in the biblical revelation of God (v. 20).

But, Paul argues, it is not in the law one should trust, for sin reigns despite the law. "You therefore who teach another, do you not teach yourself? You who preach that one should not steal, do you steal? You who say that one must not commit adultery, do you commit adultery [see John 8:11]? You who abhor idols, do you rob temples?" (vv. 21-23). The great wrong in the life of this Jew was that while he boasted in the law and boasted of relationship to God, he dishonored God by "breaking the Law" (v. 23) and brought God's reputation to nothing in the eyes of the Gentiles (v. 24).

CIRCUMCISION AND KEEPING THE LAW (2:25-29)

Why be a Jew at all? Truly to be a Jew is to obey God in faith from the heart (v. 29). His outward sign (circumcision) of the covenant relationship cannot shield him from the wrath of God. Circumcision was only a visible seal of a true heart relationship to God of love and obedience (Deut. 30:6; Rom. 4:11). Some Jews mistook the seal for the reality. When they evidenced by their breaking of God's law that the reality was not there, God invalidated the sealing significance of the rite (v. 25).

On the other hand, when a person does not have the seal but demonstrates by loving obedience to God and His will that he possesses the inward reality, his uncircumcision by nature will be counted by God as if he were circumcised and in covenant relationship (v. 26). The word Jew means "praise" (Gen. 29:35). Paul states that the true Jew is not the one who glories and trusts in the outward appearance of circumcision or in the listening to the law and legalistically following its precepts. The true Jew is one who in his heart has entered into a relationship with God of humble response (faith) to God's gracious love and election (Deut. 10:16). Such a one looks to God for His praise, and not to men.

Paul is not actually arguing that Gentiles who fulfill the intent of the law become true Jews (despite much appeal to these verses to the contrary). He is speaking to his fellow countrymen (v. 17) to the effect that the real significance of a Jew lies in his relationship to God, and not in his nationality or religious heritage. Although it is true that Paul says, "If therefore the uncircumcised man [Gentile] keep the requirements of the Law, will not his uncircumcision be regarded as circumcision [covenant relationship to God]?" (v. 26), he does not go so far here or elsewhere (on Gal. 6:16 see chap. 8, note 25) to call Gentiles true Jews. "Circumcision . . . of the heart" (v. 29) refers to true repentance before God (Jer. 4:4); "by the Spirit, not by the letter" either has reference to the Holy Spirit's work or to the inward spiritual relationship to God contrasted with the mere performance of the rite (1:9); "his praise is not from men, but from God" (v. 29) picks up the thought of verse 17 ("name 'Jew' ") and excludes all criticism of others based on pride of superiority. Thus the truth is established that it is the spirit of the law that is efficacious, not its mere outward forms and ritual performance.

THE ADVANTAGE OF THE JEW (3:1-8)

Is there then any advantage *at all* in being a Jew and having circumcision (3:1)? The answer expected from what Paul has just said might appear to be no. But rather he says, "Great in every respect" (3:2). "First" (Gk. *prōton*) anticipates a list of advantages, but Paul gets sidetracked and gives only the first and no doubt the most important reason: because "they were entrusted with the oracles of God" (3:2). Although the "oracles" (Gk. *logia,* words or pronouncements) of God may refer to the whole Old Testament revelation of God in the Bible, from verse 3 it may be inferred that the Abrahamic and prophetic promises of a Messiah are prominent (see also Acts 7:38; Heb. 5:12, 1 Pet. 4:11). What Paul is saying is that this revealed salvation-history (oracles) was of tremendous advantage to the Jew in that it gave him a special understanding of God, man's condition, the salvation of God, His will, the promises of the coming of the Christ (Luke 24:44), and the Abrahamic promises confirmed by the prophets.[34]

There now follow three objections to Paul's thesis that the Jews do have an advantage in the Word of God given to them (3:3-8). Perhaps by listing them together with Paul's answers they can be seen more clearly:

> Objection Number 1 (implied): "The Jews have disbelieved these (Abrahamic and Messianic) promises."
> Answer: "What then? If some did not believe . . ." (vv. 3-4).

---

34. For a very convincing case that uppermost in Paul's mind was the Abrahamic covenant promises, which included the Messianic promise ("in you all the families of the earth shall be blessed," Gen. 12:3; see Gal. 3:8, 16), see Sam K. Williams, "The 'Righteousness of God' in Romans," pp. 265-68. Further, Williams argues that the terms "the faithfulness of God" (v. 3), "the righteousness of God" (v. 5), and "the truth of God" (v. 7) are virtual equivalents throughout the whole epistle.

Objection Number 2: "But if our unrighteousness demonstrates . . ." (v. 5).

Answer: "May it never be! For otherwise how will God
judge?" (v. 6)

Objection Number 3: "But if through my lie . . ." (vv.
7-8).

Answer: "Their condemnation is just" (v. 8).

The first objection touches on the problem of the unbelief
of Israel in the Abrahamic and prophetic promises of the
Messiah that Paul later develops in detail (chaps. 9-11). How
is Israel's possession of the oracles of God any advantage if
they don't believe them? Israel has been and is now the trustee
of the divine Word that God wills the salvation of all peoples
on the basis of faith. Perhaps the Words of God are not really
reliable after all. Paul's answer is that the unbelief of "some"
(not all) does not nullify the reliability of God's Words. Nor
does such unbelief cancel the great advantages to the nation
of possession of the knowledge of God in the Scriptures and
of being a covenant people. Can man's lack of response to
God's promises (unbelief) cancel out His faithfulness (and
make Him a liar) to His own divine plan announced to
Abraham?

In verse 4, after reacting with abhorrence to such a
thought, Paul adds a further statement about the relationship
of God's faithfulness to man's sin and includes a reference to
Psalm 51. "May it never be![35] Rather, let God be found true,
though every man be found a liar . . . that thou mightest be
justified." Even if *all* (not just some) were to disbelieve God's
Words, it would only serve to highlight the truth and
faithfulness of God. For example, David declares that his sin,

35. The expression in the Greek (*mē genoito*) literally translated means
"perish the thought!" or "may it not be!" However, since in the Greek
OT (LXX) this same expression is used in connection with the name of
God (1 Sam. 24:6; 26:11; 1 Kings 21:3), the KJV translation, which adds
the stronger idea of God's abhorrence ("God forbid"), is to be preferred
(John Murray, *The Epistle to the Romans,* 1:94 n. 1).

rather than making God unjust for condemning him, has vin-
dicated God's justice (Ps. 51:4). If sin does not disestablish
God's justice, then neither can man's unbelief cancel out
God's faithfulness and truthfulness.

This approach of Paul raises further objections concerning
how God can be just in condemning the sinner when his sin
really serves to establish the righteousness of God (v. 5).[36]
Paul answers again in abhorrence of the thought and appeals
to God's moral government of the world: "How will God
judge the world?" (v. 6).

Further, it is objected, if God gets glory through sin, why
not go on sinning and bring more glory to God (v. 7)? At this
point Paul dismisses the question with a rather rude slap
across the cheek, "Their condemnation [judgment] is just"
(v. 8)—that is, the judgment of all those who object to being
judged as sinners. But he will return to these moral problems
again later on in the letter (chaps. 6 and 9-11).

Paul has shown that the man with the knowledge of God in
the Bible stands equally under God's wrath with the pagan.
He has no advantage before God's judgment. Such a man
demonstrates by his judgment of the pagan that he knows
what is right, yet by his own life he shows that his relationship
to God is all external and formal, not personal and real. The
great advantage of possessing the Bible's promises is not invalidated by any amount of unbelief. God's promises remain
true regardless of man's rejection.

CONCLUSION: MORAL GUILT OF THE WHOLE WORLD

3:9-20

In this final paragraph of the long section dealing with
mankind's condition under the judgment of God (1:18—
3:20), Paul concludes by bringing both the sinner without the
Bible (1:18-32) and the sinner with the Bible (2:1—3:8)

---

36. "I am speaking in human terms" means simply that he is adopting the
     diatribe method of interjecting objections opposed to his views so that he
     might further clarify his teaching.

together as equally "under sin" (3:9). The Jew (or moralist) is no better off than the pagan. Both are equally guilty before God. Paul appeals to the statements of the Old Testament Scriptures concerning both Jews and Gentiles (vv. 10-18) and concludes that man is universally and totally affected by rebellion against God (vv. 19-20).[37]

THE CHARGE (3:9)

"What then [does this argument amount to]? Are we [Jews] better [off] than they [the pagan Gentiles]? Not in every respect."[38] It might be inferred from Paul's statements in verse 2 that the Jew was in a better position in regard to judgment than the pagan because he had the advantage of the oracles of God. But Paul says the opposite is true. Although the Jew has a great advantage in every other way, in one respect he does not, that is, in judgment for sin. He adds that he has already "charged" (Gk. *proaitiaomai*) that both are "under sin." To be under sin means, as Paul has shown in 1:18—2:29, to be under God's wrath and judgment for sin (7:14; Gal. 3:22). It may also mean "under the power [dominion] of sin" (NEB, RSV). Paul is saying that all men (no ex-

---

37. Total depravity must not be understood to mean that all men are as bad or as depraved as they can get; or that men in this condition show no love, kindness, honesty, morality, etc., but that man is infected with rebellion against his Creator, and this rebellion has extended itself in some measure throughout our whole being. If sin were blue in color, I would be some shade of blue all over. Even in my best deeds there is a discoloration of self-centeredness instead of God-centeredness. Charles H. Spurgeon, the great English preacher, once remarked, "He who doubts total depravity had better study himself."

38. This latter sentence has two major interpretive problems in determining Paul's exact thought. The first involves the word "better" (Gr. *proechomai*), which has three possible meanings; the second involves the words "not in every respect" (Gr. *oy pantōs*), which has two different senses. We have given the sense in the above translation that seems preferable to us as well as to others (Cranfield, I:187-91; Käsemann, p. 68. Only the NEB margin seems to have this correct sense for both expressions). For the sense, "Not at all," see E. H. Gifford, "Romans," in *The Bible Commentary: New Testament*, p. 85; TDNT; RSV; Barrett, *The Epistle to the Romans*, pp. 66-69.

ceptions) are under the dominion of both the moral guilt and
the corruption of sin.

THE PROOF (3:10-18)

Paul now turns to six selective passages from the Psalms
and the book of Isaiah to demonstrate that the Bible teaches
that all men are unrighteous before God and do not acknowledge Him as Lord in their lives. They require little comment.

1. The *character* of men (vv. 10-12). In five negative
statements, Paul leaves no hope for man having a divine
spark of righteousness in him that only needs to be fanned.

2. The *conduct* of men (vv. 13-17). Men betray the inner
condition of their heart by their speech ("throat," "tongue,"
"mouth," see Matt. 12:37; Mark 7:20-21) and by their actions ("feet," "paths," "path of peace"). The heart blazes
the way, the mouth and feet follow.

3. The *cause* of their conduct is put last (v. 18): "There is
no fear of God before his eyes" (Ps. 36:1).

THE CONCLUSION (3:19-20)

The Jew, of course, might think to escape from the force of
these quotations from his own Bible by insisting that they
refer to pagans and not to the Jewish covenant people.
Although even a careful study of the context of the quotes
shows otherwise, Paul responds somewhat differently by
reminding the objector that "whatever the Law says, it speaks
to those who are under the Law." This revelation in the Old
Testament law (whole OT)[39] that reveals the universal sin of
all mankind before God also declares the judgment of God
equally upon both Jew and pagan.

The twofold purpose for which the Old Testament declared
this judgment was: (1) that no man, whether Jew or pagan,
may plead before God any righteousness of his own: "That

39. The "law" (as in chaps. 2 and 3) refers not only to the Mosaic codes but
    also to the prophets and Psalms, i.e., the whole OT (F. F. Bruce, *The
    Epistle of Paul to the Romans* [Grand Rapids: Eerdmans, 1963], p. 99).

every mouth may be closed" (Gk. *phrassō*, shut up), or as Phillips puts it: "that every excuse may die on the lips of him who makes it"; and (2) that the whole human race (world) should "become accountable to God." The law then cannot be used as an excuse or repose. Man must be silent and confess that he is a sinner: "It is the straight-edge of the Law that shows us how crooked we are" (Phillips).

But why did the Old Testament speak in this harsh manner about man? Because God must reveal to him his true condition before Him, the Creator, that he has no righteousness of his own. A man must, then, abandon law works[40] as a means of acceptance before God: "By the works of the Law no flesh will be justified in His sight" (v. 20) The psalmist exclaims, "If Thou, Lord, shouldst mark iniquities, O Lord, who could stand?" (Ps. 130:3). Therefore the proper response before God is to invite God to *not* "enter into judgment with Thy servant, for in Thy sight no man living is righteous" (Ps. 143:2). The first true function of the law (whether of Moses or the prophets) is to unmask us and show us that we are sinners ("knowledge of sin") and that it is impossible to be accepted before God on the basis of keeping the law. But can we accept this exposure?

According to Hans Christian Anderson's famous tale, certain clever swindlers approached an emperor offering to weave for him a rare and costly garment that would have the marvelous capacity of making known to him the fools and knaves in his realm. Because of the magical quality of the threads, the garment would be invisible to all but the wise and pure in heart. Delighted, the emperor commissioned the weaving of the royal robes at great cost, only to find, to his dismay, that he obviously was a fool and knave, for he saw nothing on the looms. On the day set for the grand parade, the clever swindlers collected their royal fee, dressed the emperor in his potbellied nakedness, and skipped out of town

---

40. "Works of the Law" are not merely good works but carry the added significance of works done in obedience to the law and *regarded as, in themselves,* a means of justification.

as the parade began. The whole populace joined the courtiers in praising the king's garments, none daring to admit that they saw nothing but the emperor's nudity, lest they be branded as self-admitted fools and knaves. The entire parade of folly collapsed, however, as the shame of king and people was exposed by a child's honest remark, "The emperor has no clothes!"

Neither the king nor his subjects were admitting his nakedness until the boy's truth destroyed their lie, ripping away their fig leaf of common hypocrisy. Thus, everyone's pride was hurt, and everyone's shame was exposed. Likewise, so long as men live under the illusion that they are righteous in themselves and refuse to acknowledge the folly of their sinfulness in the presence of the truth of God's revelation, there can be no appreciation of the gospel that Paul preaches. It is not enough to admit that man (emperor) has no outer clothing. We must see that whether we have the knowledge of the Bible or do not know the Bible, in the sight of God we are absolutely naked! It is not merely that we have committed sins (partially unclothed), but we must see ourselves as sinful before God and in rebellion (totally unclothed), completely incapable in ourselves of providing any acceptable clothing (righteousness) in the sight of our Creator.

Man has, in rebelling, suppressed the truth of his creaturehood revealed in the external nature of his existence (vv. 20-23). He has also rebelled against God's law in his inward nature by violating his conscience (2:14-15). Sin, as Paul has explained, is basically a wrong relationship to God; it is active or passive rebellion against His lordship over our lives; it is a power controlling us. This is the Bible's concept of man's sin that leaves him without excuse and under the judgment and wrath of God. Man's predicament renders him hopeless unless God has found some other means of accepting sinful men apart from either law works or religious rites. Will He give man righteousness? How will He do it and still remain just and holy?

3

THE GOOD NEWS: THE GIFT OF RIGHTEOUSNESS BY FAITH

3:21—4:25

Thankfully, God's word of judgment is not His only word. "But now" (v. 21), Paul says, something utterly new has entered human history. This is the great turning point of the letter. All that man has been able to accomplish stands justly under God's wrath. But our own need is met by God's intervention in mercy and grace through Jesus Christ. Now *God's* righteousness affecting man's salvation has been revealed as a free gift to the guilty. It is obtained solely on the basis of faith in Jesus Christ apart from any moralistic works (3:21-26). Therefore, all meritorious boasting in works is excluded by the principle of complete trust in Jesus Christ for acceptance before God (3:27-31). This faith method of salvation taught in the good news of the gospel is in fact the very one revealed in the Old Testament and illustrated beautifully and irrefutably by the lives of Abraham and David (4:1-25).

GOD'S PROVISION: THE GIFT OF RIGHTEOUSNESS

3:21-31

This section has been called "the heart of the epistle and of the Pauline message." In the brief span of a few verses, Paul sets forth God's finished plan and how He dealt with the sinful human condition. Since Paul compresses such a tremendous amount of truth into a brief section, we will need to examine and enlarge (from other Pauline passages) upon a number of the key words found here, such as redemption, grace, justification, faith, and propitiation. Paul's precise thought is also revealed by his use of about twenty independent prepositions and eight prepositions compounded with other words. These syntactical relationships are difficult to explain in a brief commentary, but one should be aware that there is far more in the text than the word meanings.

In short, Paul teaches that what man could not effect for himself (righteousness) because he is under the wrath of God, God has provided as a free gift through faith in Jesus Christ. The actual historical and public crucifixion of the young Jewish carpenter, Jesus of Nazareth, reveals God's righteousness and provides the basis for this full forgiveness and deliverance from God's wrath of all who put their trust in God's Son (1:16). Paul refers to the death of Jesus in the language of the Old Testament sacrificial system (vv. 24-25). Since God's deliverance comes to us solely by faith, there can be no place for boasting or self-congratulation (vv. 27-30).

THIS RIGHTEOUSNESS IS NOT BY THE LAW (3:21)

Paul likes to speak paradoxically: "apart from the Law" and yet "being witnessed by the Law and the prophets."[1] It has already been shown by Paul that law-righteousness (legalism) rests upon human achievement and, because of our self-centered nature, leads to God's wrath (4:15). So God's righteousness must be manifested in a different way so as to lead to our justification. On the other hand, the law (OT) itself, if we correctly understand it, points in the same direction (3:31). In the *law* Abraham and David (chap. 4) are illustrations of how God's gift-righteousness came to men of old through faith. Paul has already referred to Habakkuk 2:4 from the prophets (1:17). Paul's rich use of the word *law*

---

1. "The law and the prophets" probably refers to the whole OT in a two-fold division. Such a division is found in the Qumran *Manual of Discipline,* Zadokite fragments, and other Qumran literature (Laird Harris, "What Books Belong in the Canon of Scripture?" in *Can I Trust My Bible?* ed. H. Vos [Chicago: Moody, 1968], p. 76).

(*nomos*) should not be overlooked. Here Paul stresses that the righteousness of God comes not by legalism (law), yet the law (OT) as God's revelation witnesses to the importance of faith.

The "righteousness of God" once again comes before us. Paul has in 1:17 related this term to the gospel and the power of God working salvation to all who believe. The reader is referred to that passage for further help and to the discussion under justification (3:24).

THIS RIGHTEOUSNESS IS THE RIGHTEOUSNESS OF FAITH (3:22-23)

As in 1:17, Paul immediately links this saving activity with man's faith. Most commentators see both of the following expressions related to this same truth: "through faith in Jesus Christ" and "for all those who believe" (v. 22). However, the two expressions so understood seem redundant. Therefore, some see the expression "through faith in Jesus Christ" as a reference to Jesus' own faithfulness to God. They translate the term as "through the faithfulness of Christ" and understand it to mean that through Christ's faithfulness and obedience, God has manifested his saving grace, which allows all nations to stand, justified by faith, before God.[2]

"There is no distinction" (e.g., between Jew and Gentile, those with the knowledge of the Bible and those without the knowledge of the Bible, moralist and pornographer), "for all have sinned" (v. 23). They have sinned in the sense of Paul's concept of sin in 1:18—3:20, namely, that regardless of the differences among men in respect to the kind and intensity of their offenses against God's law, all without exception are in the category of rebellious sinners ("under sin," 3:9). They have willfully suppressed the outward and inward knowledge of God, who claims as Creator to be Lord of their lives. In doing this, they "fall short of the glory of God."

The tenses in the two verbs are important. All "have

2. Sam K. Williams, "The Righteousness of God in Romans," pp. 274-76; also Richard N. Longenecker, *Paul, Apostle of Liberty,* pp. 149-52.

sinned" (Greek past tense)[3] and "fall short" (present tense).
The historical fact of man's continued sinful condition leads
to his present falling short or "lack" (Gk. *hystereō*, "in need
of") of the "glory of God." God created man in His own image that in dependence upon Him, man might reflect the
Creator's own personal and moral excellence. Sin breaks
man's relationship with God and fractures the full imaging
activity of the creature. Jesus Christ, as man, perfectly
reflected the invisible God (Heb. 1:3). Through Him, sinful
men are restored to the fully intended image and glory of God
(2 Cor. 3:18; Col. 3:10).

THE DIVINE PLAN OF COMMUNICATING THIS RIGHTEOUSNESS TO MAN
(3:24-26)

How does God actually provide this grace-gift of His saving righteousness? What role does Jesus Christ, and His
death, play in this plan? Can even God account a sinful man
as being righteous? How is God's gift attained? Some comment on each of the key words in verses 24-25 may help to il-
luminate the apostle's thoughts on these questions.

1. *Justification* (v. 24). What does Paul mean by being
justified? Considerable discussion has revolved around attempted definitions of this concept. It is without doubt the
key theme of the whole epistle. The Greek verb translated
"justify" (*dikaioō*) has exactly the same stem as the Greek
noun for "righteousness" (*dikaiosynē*). To justify someone,
then, would logically mean to make someone righteous in the
sense of infusing goodness. Although Chrysostom (A.D. 407)
and the church likewise followed this view for centuries, it is
now generally held to be wrong (an exception being some

3. The aorist tense of this verb has been unwisely limited by some interpreters to refer to participation in Adam's sin. However, the complexive
   (constative) aorist may simply view many acts as a whole (F. Blass and A.
   Debrunner, *A Greek Grammar of the New Testament and Other Early
   Christian Literature,* par. 332, p. 171). In this case the past tense is simply gathering the whole human race under one canopy of sinfulness.
   "Sinned" is the Greek word *hamartanō,* which literally means in
   classical Greek "to miss the mark" but in biblical literature refers to
   rebellion against God or to transgression of His will.

Roman Catholics). Even from one consideration alone this view is questionable. In the epistles, frequent mention is made of Christians who are not entirely ethically good (righteous), yet are nevertheless justified (e.g., 1 Cor. 3:3, 6:11).

In its place is offered the rendering to "declare [or treat] as righteous."[4] This idea suggests that God now views the sinner as if he were righteous (good) or had never sinned. While this rendering escapes the difficulty of asserting that in justification men are infused with ethical righteousness, it likewise flounders on linguistic and theological grounds. If God *treated* as ethically righteous those who were not morally righteous, would this not be a sort of legal fiction? Can even God pretend that black is white or that bad is good?

It is far better and more in harmony with Paul's whole teaching to understand justification to mean *to make righteous*.[5] At the same time, it is necessary to recognize that "righteous" (in this instance) has no reference to ethical goodness or virtue, but means *right, clear, acquitted* in God's court.[6] Justification, then, is God's activity in behalf of guilty

---

4. Verbs ending in $o\overline{o}$ in Greek (if they are verbs of mental perception or connected to adjectives denoting moral qualities) denote not the making but the counting or deeming of the specific moral quality (C. K. Barrett, *The Epistle to the Romans,* p. 75). This is usually called the *forensic* (court room) use.

5. As Paul's concept of righteousness was drawn from the OT word usage rather than the Greek, so must we see his concept of justification. In the Hebrew OT the equivalent word lying behind "justify" is *tsadak,* which primarily means to "cause to be righteous," that is, *show* to be righteous. It cannot mean to "treat *as if* righteous."

6. Further support for this idea is seen in the fact that the opposite of justification is *not unrighteousness* (1:18-19), which would make justification right living, but *condemnation* (Rom. 5:18; 8:34; see Barrett, p. 75 and TDNT). Justification, then, is that act of God whereby He acquits us (1 Cor. 4:4) of our moral guilt before Him (under wrath) and through grace puts us in a radically different relationship to Him and all His benefits. Perhaps the *Good News for Modern Man* (TEV) captures the thought when it translates: "they are put right with him through Jesus Christ." Hence, justification means basically *standing* with God. It is neither ethical righteousness imputed (KJV) nor imparted but is a status conferred on the ground of faith, not on the ground of merit (see Leon Morris, *The Apostolic Preaching of the Cross* [Grand Rapids: Eerdmans, 1956], chaps. 7 and 8, for a full discussion).

sinners whereby He goes forth in power to *forgive* and *deliver* them in the present time from judgment by His grace, to declare a *new reality* to exist, and to *transform* and *empower* them so that they can act to become what they are in the new reality. It is more than—but certainly includes—the mere forensic (legal acquittal) act of God. God actually works to forgive the sinner (4:5), to place him in a whole radically different relationship to Himself (5:2), and to give him power to become righteous before God. In this new relationship we receive enablement through the Holy Spirit, who brings the lordship of Jesus Christ to bear on our lives (8:1-9), to worship and serve God in His will (holiness).[7]

This justification Paul further qualifies by the word "as a gift" (Gk. *dōrean,* "for nothing"). This same word is found in John 15:25, where Jesus says, "They hated Me without a cause," and in Galatians 2:21, "then Christ died needlessly" (i.e., for nothing). It is plain, then, that by this word Paul is stressing the gift aspect of God's method of putting us right with Himself. We are acquitted (forgiven and introduced to salvation) for no cause or reason in us, that is, we have no merit or virtue, nor is any required (Phil. 3:9).

2. *Grace* (v. 24). The reason why sinners, though guilty, can be justified lies in God's grace. This is a key word of Paul's in all his epistles (he uses it 100 times). In the succeeding chapters this element will be a primary point as he discusses the new life imparted through justification (5:2). Grace (Gk. *charis*) is the free and unmerited favor of God. It is that aspect of God's love that leads Him to bestow on men His free forgiveness even while they are rebellious sinners (5:8; Eph. 2:8). Grace, however, is more than God's favorable attitude toward us; it includes also the activity and divine provi-

---

7. The present tense of the participle translated "being justified" stresses that justification is a *present experience* for all those who are needing the glory of God restored to their lives (v. 23). For the Jews in Paul's day, justification was always future, awaiting the balancing of the good works against the evil works of each man (TDNT). The teaching of Jesus (Luke 18:4), as well as Paul's, was radically different at this point. This viewpoint has recently been challenged in E. P. Sanders, *Paul and Palestinian Judaism,* p. 494, who argues that *present* righteousness is also a concept of Judaism.

sions for living fully in the new relationship (Rom. 5:21; 1 Cor. 15:10; 2 Cor. 12:9). When Paul wants to stress that salvation arises from God's initiative and not from man's work, he uses the word *grace* (11:6).

God's grace, although free to the sinner, cannot be made a "cheap" grace, because it cost God the tremendous price of the death of His own Son. What has cost God so much cannot be cheap for us. Costly grace confronts us with a call to relinquish our very lives and submit absolutely to the obedience of Christ.[8]

G. Campbell Morgan used to relate an experience he had while preaching this message of free forgiveness in a small mining town in the Midwest. Following the service, a miner came up and argued that this kind of salvation was too cheap. Morgan asked him how he got to work each day. The miner replied, "I walk. I live close to the mine." "How do you get down in the mine shaft?" Morgan asked. "I ride the elevator," the miner said. Morgan continued, "How much does it cost you?" "Nothing, it's free for us miners," he said. "Well," replied Morgan, "it must be a cheap operation then!" "No," said the miner, "it's free for us, but it cost the company a lot." Then suddenly, as if a light had dawned, he exclaimed, "Oh, my God, now I see it. Salvation's free for me, but it cost the company a lot, all that God had!"[9]

The important question here is whether grace is purely arbitrary, or whether it rests in some decisive judicial act of God that allows Him to maintain His own holy standards and yet to acquit and deliver sinners.

3. *Redemption* (v. 24). Paul's answer to this question lies in understanding the death of Jesus as a sacrificial death. Two words drawn from the Old Testament highlight this. "Redemption" (Gk. *apolytrōsis*) means basically to buy a slave out of bondage in order to set him free. This imagery arises from both the Old Testament concept of the redemption of

---

8. Dietrich Bonhoeffer, *Cost of Discipleship* (New York: Macmillan, 1959), chap. 1.
9. G. Campbell Morgan, *Westminster Pulpit* (Westwood, N.J.: Revell, n.d.), 9:120-33.

the nation Israel from slavery in Egypt (Ex. 6:6; 15:13) and
from the Passover lamb sacrifice (Ex. 12; 1 Cor. 5:7).

Slavery produced a human condition from which a man
could not free himself. It was hopeless unless someone from
outside would willingly intervene and pay the price to free
him. The release of the Viet Nam prisoners of war and the
Iranian hostages may form a close modern parallel. The imagery depicts the evil plight in which man finds himself as a
result of his sin. He is in a state of imprisonment from which
he cannot break free. He is helplessly under the judgment of
God. But God Himself has intervened, paid the price, and effected the release. From the reference to "blood" in verse 25,
the price paid can be nothing else than the death of Christ
(Mark 10:45; Gal. 3:13; 1 Pet. 1:18).[10] Christ's death provided
the required ransom price to free men from the captivity and
dominion of sin and liberate them to do the will of God. Jesus
of Nazareth is Himself the ransom (1 Cor. 1:30; Titus 2:14).

4. *Propitiation* (v. 25). Paul immediately links the redemption effected through Christ with the concept of "a propitiation effected through Christ with the concept of "a propitiation in His blood through faith." "Propitiation" (Gk.
hilastērion)[11] must be understood in the light of the context of

10. There are at least six different Greek words used for "redemption" in the
NT (Morris, chap. 1). Paul does not say to whom the price was paid nor
exactly how Christ's death provided this tremendous effect. There can be
little doubt, however, that Paul's thought included the idea of substitutionary death (Gal. 3:13-14).

11. The concept is fraught with problems both linguistically and theologically. *Theologically,* there are two views: the *first,* as in the NASB, NIV
(margin), and KJV, sees the term denoting a true sense of propitiation
(satisfaction assuaging God's holy wrath against sin); and the *second,* as
in the RSV, which regards the word as conveying only the thought of
"expiation" (wipe out sin, removal of guilt). The two concepts are difficult to distinguish, but the former, more in agreement with Paul's argument, stresses specifically the wrath of God that is personally appeased
by the sacrificial death of Christ (So C. E. B. Cranfield, *A Critical and
Exegetical Commentary on the Epistle to the Romans,* 1:214-17).
Linguistically, the word may be either a noun or an adjective. As a *noun*
it could mean "mercy seat" (LXX word 22 times for the golden lid of the
ark where the blood was applied, Ex. 25:21; also Heb. 9:5) or "propitiation" (or "propitiatory victim" [Cranfield]); as an *adjective,* the thought
would be "a means of propitiation." Morris argues cogently for the latter (p. 172); F. F. Bruce (*The Epistle of Paul to the Romans,* p. 105) for
the former position. It is difficult to settle.

Paul's argument in 1:18—3:20. He has established that there is a real wrath of God that extends to all men because of their own willful suppression of the truth of His claims as Creator and Judge. In this context, Paul shows that in the historical death of Jesus ("in His blood"), this wrath (anger) of God found adequate judicial *satisfaction*.

God condones nothing because of His holy and righteous nature. Since sin deserves punishment and death (1:32; 6:23), there can be no reconciliation without judicial satisfaction. It cannot be far from the truth if we see in the death of Jesus a substitution (2 Cor. 5:21; 1 Pet. 2:24). He, the righteous one (yet fully human), suffered the just penalty (wrath) for our sins that God might still remain just and the One who can fully pardon the guilty sinner (v. 26). The marvel consists in the act of God's grace, where in infinite and consuming love He himself provided the costly satisfaction (propitiation) that we in ourselves were incapable of presenting (Rom. 5:8; Titus 3:4; 1 John 4:9-10). Something of this heart of God was captured by Elizabeth C. Clephane when she wrote,

> And though the road be rough and steep,
> I go to the desert to find my sheep.
> But none of the ransomed ever knew
> How deep were the waters crossed,
> Nor how dark was the night that the Lord passed through
> Ere He found His sheep that was lost.

The only adequate response to such love and grace is obedient faith. When one forsakes all his own works and former loyalties and casts himself totally upon Jesus Christ as God's propitiatory gift-sacrifice for his sin, he believes, in the biblical sense. At that point the saving righteousness of God becomes effective in his life (4:16-25).

But, Paul, why did Jesus have to die in order to reveal God's righteousness in the gospel? In verses 25-26 Paul attempts to answer this question. Jesus' propitiatory death first shows that God is really morally righteous. God showed restraint (forbearance; Gk. *anochē,* Rom. 2:4) in not visiting wrath upon men's sins in the past ages before Christ came when "He passed over" (v. 25) their sins (not "remission" as in KJV). Yet it was not due to moral indifference toward sin that He restrained Himself. Though the "sins previously committed" may be understood as sins in a person's life before one becomes a Christian,[12] most understand Paul to refer to the sins of men in *former ages* before the governmental act of God occurred in Jesus' death. In days past God did not exercise His full wrath on men for their sins; He was patient and merciful with men (Acts 14:16; 17:30). But in Jesus' death God manifested the truth that He was yet not any less wrathful against sin. The supreme penalty for our sins was borne by Jesus. This allows God to remain God—morally perfect—and yet forgive and receive sinners.

So, too, in the present, God's justice and holy hatred of sin are still maintained even when He, in grace through the gospel, takes sinners and puts them in right standing with Himself. Jesus' death vindicates the moral character of God (v. 26). Again (as in v. 24) Paul stresses the present tense of justification, "and the justifer (one who *is* justifying) of the one who has faith in Jesus." He wants to emphasize not only that justification occurs now in this life, but also the idea of God's continual *empowering* of us to *be righteous*. Isaac Watts's familiar hymn captures well the sinner's response to such grace:

> When I survey the wondrous cross
> On which the Prince of glory died,
> My richest gain I count but loss,
> And pour contempt on all my pride.
>
> Were the whole realm of nature mine,
> That were a present far too small:
> Love so amazing, so divine,
> Demands my soul, my life, my all.

---

12. C. A. Anderson Scott, *Christianity According to St. Paul* (New York: Cambridge U., n.d.), pp. 64ff.

THE RESULTS OF GOD'S PLAN (3:27-31)

There are two results of this "faith alone" plan of justification. First, it excludes boasting (vv. 27-28). All boasting depends upon some supposed superiority earned through a system of good works (ethical and religious)—that is, pride of accomplishment. The faith system, on the other hand, depends totally on the merciful act of God in Jesus Christ's death. Since God acting in *grace* has done everything, there can be no grounds for human accomplishment. As D. T. Niles has so well put it, "Christianity is simply one beggar telling another beggar where he found bread." If heaven is to be a place where we go because of our good works, we would turn it into hell by going around—as we surely would—boasting of all we did to get there.

Second, this plan of salvation by faith alone establishes the true unity of God as God over all men (vv. 29-30). The Jew would be the first to confess that God is one (*shema,* Deut. 6:4). How, then, Paul argues, could He be the one God of both Jews and Gentiles unless He had a plan of righting men with Himself that did not require all men to be Jews (circumcised)? This plan is the faith plan that is equally valid for Jews (circumcised) and the Gentiles (uncircumcised).

But, Paul, doesn't what you have said about the faith plan (3:21-30) cancel out the law of God entirely? Paul answers emphatically, no (v. 31). In fact what he has said rather serves to "establish" (confirm, hold valid) the law. While Paul could mean by the word *law* the whole Old Testament (3:19),[13] the more immediate context (faith versus works of law) favors a slightly different view. He probably refers to the charge that by his gospel of grace he is allegedly setting aside the moral commands in the law. Since antinomian (no obligation to keep the moral law) charges against Paul are later raised and dealt with in detail by the apostle (chaps. 6-8), it is

13. Paul's discussion of the faith of Abraham and of David (chap. 4) would then be taken as a proof of this assertion (see H. P. Liddon, *An Explanatory Analysis of St. Paul's Epistle to the Romans,* pp. 69-70; Barrett, *The Epistle to the Romans,* 84; Bruce, p. 109).

likely that he here simply makes the flat statement that the righteousness of God revealed in the gospel fully agrees with the moral nature of God revealed in the commandments of the Old Testament.

These verses (vv. 27-31) bring to a close the most crucial and concentrated argument of the whole letter (1:18—3:31). Before proceeding, it might be well to summarize briefly the two main focal points.

First, Paul has described the human situation from the divine perspective. Men, whether religious or irreligious, moral or immoral, have chosen to glorify themselves rather than their Creator. The man without the knowledge of God in the Bible asserts himself in the form of rebellion against the natural order and his conscience and by so doing claims freedom from God, only to find that in the end he debases himself and becomes inhuman. On the other hand, the religious cultured man with the knowledge of God in the Bible—or at least a sense of morality—asserts his rebellion by, in pride, refusing to repent before God. By substituting the worship of his own self-righteousness, he has failed to keep the true spirit of the Bible, which is inward humble submission and obedience to the God of the Bible. Both kinds of people are equally under God's judicial wrath.

Second, all hope is not lost, because God has Himself powerfully acted in history for the acquittal of the guilty. His holy wrath against man's sin was meted out to Jesus Christ in His propitiatory death on the cross. God shows thereby that He is fully just and able to put in the right all sinners who trust in Jesus Christ. To explain this good news, Paul has pressed into service the language of the law court (justify), slave market (redemption), and the temple (propitiation). Men put their trust in God's act in Jesus Christ and experience full pardon, deliverance from sin, and a new standing before God. In the remainder of the epistle, Paul will show the implications of this new status before God as it relates to many different situations.

ABRAHAM AND JUSTIFICATION BY FAITH

4:1-25

Paul has established the principle that faith alone secures right standing before God, not works of human achievement (3:21-31). He has declared (3:27) that the faith system revealed in the gospel excludes all boasting based upon human achievement. God considers the faith of an individual, not circumcision, as the ground for justification. Chapter 4 expands further on these points and concludes Paul's major point on justification.

As far as the Jew was concerned, any discussion of the correct approach to God must consider Abraham, the father of Israel. Abraham is depicted in Jewish thought as having performed the whole law before it was given. He was viewed as the perfect example of all Jewish virtues.[14] Thus the case of Abraham was paramount. If he was not justified by works, then no man could be; if he was justified by faith, there can be no other justification for man. This chapter contains one of the most important discussions in the Bible concerning the relationship between faith and works. We will want to note very carefully the helpful material Paul relates toward the end of chapter 4 stating the more exact nature of faith.

Paul shows that Abraham was justified by faith and not by works, as was also David (vv. 1-8). Since Abraham's circumcision postdated his justification before God, it could not have caused his acceptance (vv. 9-12). Furthermore, the promise given to Abraham, that in his seed all nations would be blessed, was given through the righteousness of faith and had nothing to do with the law (vv. 13-22). Finally, Paul argues that the same God who justified Abraham by faith likewise through faith justifies us in Jesus Christ, who died for our sins and rose again for justification (vv. 23-25).

14. Jubilees 23:10: "Abraham was perfect in all his deeds with the Lord, and well-pleasing in righteousness all the days of his life." In Kiddushim 4:14: "We find that Abraham our father had performed the whole law before it was given" (cited by Cranfield, 1:227).

ABRAHAM AND JUSTIFICATION (4:1-8)

Paul begins with an objection to his whole view of justification. Paul, you say faith alone justifies before God, and therefore all boasting is excluded. What about our father, Abraham? Wouldn't virtuous Abraham, if he were in fact justified by works (as the rabbis teach), have something to boast about? Paul replies, Yes, he would, but in fact, before God, Abraham has no such grounds for boasting. Whatever you were taught about Abraham's boasting, forget it. The Scripture settles the issue when it says, "Abraham believed God, and it was reckoned to him as righteousness" (Rom. 4:3; Gen. 15:6).[15]

Current Jewish understanding of faith included the idea of meritorious work. Paul interprets the Genesis passage in a fresh light (vv. 4-8). First, he links together two pairs of opposites. "Works" and "due" are linked and set off in opposition to "faith" and "favor" (literally, grace). One who works gets paid, but one who does not work (and yet gets wages) must be "reckoned" (counted) as having gotten pay as a gift. Since Genesis says Abraham had righteousness "reckoned" to him (Rom. 4:11), it follows he must have received righteousness as a "favor" (gift by grace) and not as a result of his works. As Abraham, so the one "who does not work, but believes in Him who justifies [pres. tense again] the ungodly, his faith is reckoned as righteousness" (v. 5).

The reference to God justifying the "ungodly" (impious) is

15. The Greek word *logizomai* means to count, reckon, estimate, consider, ponder, credit (William F. Arndt and F. Wilbur Gingrich, *Greek-English Lexicon of the New Testament and Other Early Christian Literature* [Grand Rapids: Zondervan, 1963], s.v.). In the papyri it frequently means "to put to one's account" (James H. Moulton and George Milligan, *Vocabulary of the Greek New Testament* [Grand Rapids: Eerdmans, 1949], s.v.). The KJV in vv. 3-11 uses "count," "reckon," and "impute" all for the same verb. From v. 6 and v. 11 it is clear that what is credited to us is righteousness (right status or relationship), not faith.

unique. At least two things clearly emerge: (1) justification (and righteousness) is clearly at its initial stage a forensic (courtroom) word that does not mean "to make ethically righteous" but "to acquit" or "to grant a status of right"; and (2) since it is the ungodly (not the ethically righteous) who are justified, Paul is describing a unique divine act of grace without precedent in human affairs.[16]

Paul appeals further to Israel's great king and sweet psalmist, David (vv. 6-8). David is helpful to Paul's argument because while Abraham lived prior to the law, David was squarely under it. David, unlike Abraham, was a flagrant violator of God's law and yet was forgiven by God. Using the interpretive principle that when the same word occurs in two biblical passages, each can be used to explain the other, Paul turns to Psalm 32:1-2 to show that David also teaches justification without works.[17] The "not take into account" (not reckon) of sin mentioned by David is equivalent to "the reckoning [counting] as righteousness" in Abraham's case. Both were acquitted without works because "reckoning" belongs only to the category of favor (grace or gift) and not merit (due). At each new turn in Paul's argument it becomes clearer that justification is not the just pronouncement on

16. Jewish thought also taught that justification was a forensic act of God, but that it only occurred at the last judgment and would be a favorable verdict based on the outweighing of the good works versus bad works (Morris, p. 242). In Greek usage, "to justify the ungodly" would mean to *condemn* or punish the ungodly (TDNT). There may be an intended advance in thought between v. 7, where the plural is used ("those"), and v. 8, where the singular occurs ("the man"). If such is the case, the first line of the psalm quotation describes God's act of forgiveness that forms the basis of His judicial act of not taking our sin into account (i.e., justification). Thus God justifies the ungodly by first forgiving them, then creating a new reality. He also transforms and empowers them so that they can act and become what they already are.

17. This is a well-known rabbinical principle known technically as *gezerah shawah* (C. K. Barrett, ed., *New Testament Backgrounds,* p. 146).

human merit (Jewish view) or the imparting of goodness, but gracious forgiveness of sin and release from judgment.[18]

CIRCUMCISION AND JUSTIFICATION (4:9-12)

Paul, an objector interjects, Abraham and David were circumcised before this blessing of forgiveness could come to them, weren't they? How then can the uncircumcised ever be justified before God? Isn't it necessary to be circumcised and keep the law? (Acts 15:1).

Paul's answer revolves around the question of chronology. Abraham was in fact circumcised *after* he had been reckoned righteous: "not while circumcised, but while uncircumcised" (v. 10). He had been first acquitted by faith (Gen. 15) and circumcised (Gen. 17) about fourteen years later! Paul sees a divine purpose in this order. Abraham was to be the "father of many nations" according to the divine promise to him at the time when he believed God and was justified (Gen. 15:5; Rom. 4:17, 18). If his fatherhood consisted only in the Jewish people (circumcised), how could God fulfill the fatherhood of many nations of the promise? (vv. 17-18). But if his fatherhood consisted mainly in a lineage of those who like Abraham had received the "righteousness of faith" (v. 13), then the Gentiles (uncircumcised) could rightly be called the children of Abraham. He is first of all the father of the believing Gentiles and afterward the father of the circumcision

18. Can this section of Paul be reconciled with James 2:14-26, where James seems to argue that justification is by faith and works? In the first place, James was probably written before Romans, so it could not be an attempt to refute Paul. Second, James's use of words "justified," "works," and "faith" is not the equivalent of Paul's. In James, justification, as in Jewish thought, looks more at the *end* of one's life and whether the works done were in conjunction with real faith in Jesus Christ (see 2:1). Paul, on the other hand, views justification at the *beginning* of one's life in Christ and counts all works before that as unacceptable meritorious deeds. Works in James are like Paul's "fruit of the Spirit" (Gal. 5:22-23); while Paul calls for "a faith working through love" (Gal. 5:6), James likewise describes a "faith without works [that] is useless" (James 2:20). The essential message is the same, but the context and emphasis are different and must be carefully considered.

(Jew), providing that they "follow in the steps [lit. Gk. *stoicheō* "join the ranks"] of the faith" (v. 12). Faith is independent of circumcision.

Why, then, was Abraham circumcised at all if faith is enough? Paul explains that circumcision was a "sign" (outward token) or a "seal" (assurance, confirmation) of the "righteousness of the faith which he had [already] while uncircumcised" (v. 11). When God renewed the covenant agreement with Abraham some fourteen years after he was counted as righteous (Gen. 15), He changed his name from Abram to Abraham ("father of many nations"). As a visible seal (confirmation) that Abraham's original act of faith was accepted by God, God gave him the sign of circumcision as an evidence that he was acquitted by faith. Abraham was then to transmit this sign to a covenant people (Israel), who were to receive it as Abraham did, that is, as a seal of righteousness reckoned by faith.[19] Circumcision originally had nothing to do with works of law. Correctly understood, the rite confirms the truth of justification by faith.

PROMISE AND JUSTIFICATION (4:13-22)

Paul already alluded to the promise to Abraham that he should be the father of many nations (vv. 11-12). He elaborates further in verses 13-22 on the relationship between the promise and the law of Moses. *Promise, faith, grace,* and *heirs* are joined by Paul and put in antithesis to law (vv. 13-16). In the first place the law did not come until 430 years after the promise (Rom. 4:13; Gal. 3:17). Second, the only

19. A good illustration of this is the old twenty-dollar gold piece. The seal of the United States was imprinted on the coin as a sign that it was United States currency, but the value of the coin remained the same even if it was melted down and the seal obliterated. Now the same seal can be impressed on an iron slug, but the presence of the sign does not alter the intrinsic worthlessness of the slug. If the person who bears the sign of the circumcision (Jew) does not have the intrinsic righteousness of faith, the sign is worthless. On the other hand, if a person has the intrinsic righteousness of faith and yet lacks the sign (Gentile), he is still accepted before God.

principle that will insure the literal fulfillment of the promise
to Abraham of being a father to "many" nations (vv. 17-18)
is faith. Since only the Jews were given the law, only one nation could participate in the blessing (forgiveness of sins, vv.
7, 9)—that is, if the fulfillment of the promise depended on
the law observance. Anyway, law works wrath because of sin
and would be incompatible with the promise of blessing
(v. 15).[20]

What is promise? Promise has the same nature as grace.
His point here appears almost the same as in verses 4-5.
Promise rests on complete trust in the one who has made the
promise. It is not a legal contract where one stipulates pay for
the labor. Where labor is contracted, the man knows he will
receive his due; but where all rests on the promise of the
benefactor (grace), a man must believe to receive (as a gift)
the promised benefit (v. 16). If law provides the basis of the
inherited blessing, "faith" and "promise" have lost their
meaning (v. 14).

What is faith? Verses 17-22 help us to understand further
about the essential nature of Abraham's faith. Since this faith
is like gospel faith, it is quite important. In the first place,
Abraham's faith arose as a result of God's Word of promise
to him: "A father of many nations have I made you" (v. 17).
Authentic biblical faith only exists as response to divine
revelation (10:17).

Second, his faith was directed toward God Himself. And
Abraham's God was not unknown. He was a God "who gives
life to the dead and calls into being that which does not exist"
(v. 17). Abraham's God is a God who is the source of all life
and resurrection, the Creator. For Abraham to father a child,
when he was impotent and Sarah his wife barren, required a
God who could act and create life from the natural deadness
of the womb. Abraham, at the time of the promise of the

20. This verse has perplexed many. It certainly anticipates what Paul will
    develop further in 5:13-14. At any rate, it seems parenthetical to his main
    thought, and the rest of the argument is quite clear.

child Isaac, was about one hundred years old, and Sarah was about ninety (Gen. 17:17).

Furthermore, faith has a future aspect in that it also accepts as certain before it is fulfilled what God has promised: "In hope [in God's promise] against [human] hope he believed" (v. 18). He simply in faith took God at His Word. Abraham was "fully assured"[21] and did not waver in unbelief at the promise of God (as those who denied this doctrine of justification were doing), but he gave glory to God (vv. 20-21). He did what those in chapters 1 and 2 failed to do. Abraham acknowledged God as God, the Creator, as such altogether different from creation (holy), powerful where man is weak, living where they are dead.[22] No such trust in works of law can give this kind of glory to God. Such faith God counted as righteousness to Abraham (v. 22). Such faith He will also count as righteousness to us.

ABRAHAM'S FAITH AND GOSPEL FAITH (4:23-25)

The same kind of faith that brought righteousness without meritorious works to Abraham's account also brings righteousness to us in the gospel of Jesus Christ. This trust finds its object in the same living God of Abraham. He is the God who raised up His own Son, not from a dead womb, but from the grave (v. 24). While the faith that brings acquittal and right standing before God today is not identical in *content* to Abraham's (promise of Isaac's birth), gospel faith is the same in *quality* (nonmeritorious) and in its object (the living Creator God, who gives men promises and brings life out of death). We are asked to trust not a theological idea or generalization, but the God who acts in history and in the

---

21. Abraham's faith (and it was a biblical faith) was not based on doubt or factual uncertainty about God. This is the error of the whole neo-Protestant view of justification by faith. Faith has content and rests upon sufficient historical evidence to place it above reasonable or psychological doubt. See an excellent discussion by C. F. H. Henry, "Justification by Ignorance: A Neo-Protestant Motif?" *Journal of the Evangelical Theological Society* 13 (Winter 1970):3-14.
22. Barrett, *The Epistle to the Romans*, p. 98.

death and resurrection of Jesus. Gospel faith, like Abraham's faith, involves trust in historical acts of God.

To believe in the God who raised Jesus from the dead is also to believe in the divine explanation of that death, "Him [Jesus] who was delivered up [in death] because of [on account of] our transgressions, and was raised because of our justifcation" (v. 25).[23] Faith is not a blind leap to a God who is totally unknown. Faith trusts in the God of forgiving grace who is revealed fully in the death and resurrection of Jesus of Nazareth.

Paul has harmonized his teaching about justification with the Old Testament by explaining the account of Abraham and his faith. He has finished his main argument. Paul has talked about (1) the human situation of man under the wrath of God because of rebellion (1:18—3:20); (2) the present and future deliverance of the sinner from this wrath through the gracious and substitutionary death of Jesus (3:21-31); and finally (3) the appropriateness and indispensability of faith as the only way of securing this acquittal before God by his argument based on Abraham (chap. 4). This is truly good news.

Paul at this point turns to consider the life and human situation of those who have by faith entered into this new status of acceptance before God (chaps. 5-8). Is the life of man altered in any way by his new relationship to God? Chapters 5 through 8 can profitably be viewed as Paul's effort to show that a new life actually exists, despite certain apparent problems to the contrary.

---

23. Paul uses identical words for the parallel work of Christ in His death and resurrection. The first "because of" (our offenses) seems to carry retrospective force, i.e., "because of our transgressions" Christ was put to death. The second instance, "because of our justification," could also be retrospective. However, it seems preferable to understand the last expression as prospective, "in order that we might be justified" (Bruce, p. 119; Barrett, *The Epistle to the Romans,* p. 100; John Murray, *The Epistle to the Romans,* p. 154) In any event, no artificial separation of the effects of the death and resurrection of Christ should be entertained.

4

THE NEW SITUATION: FREEDOM
FROM THE WRATH OF GOD

5:1-21

Chapter 5 marks a turning point in Romans. Paul now assumes the reader has accepted his argument for justification by faith, and he proceeds to spell out the implications of this new relationship of grace in the lives of the justified ones. Paul shifts from argumentative to confessional style, from the second and third persons to the first, and from the indicative-declaratory tone to the subjunctive-hortatory. To accept God's free gift of righteousness also means to accept a new lordship over the life. Chapters 5 through 8 deal with the nature and effects of this radical new life in the world founded upon the "grace" in which we stand (5:2).

Because God has dealt decisively in Jesus Christ with the twin problems of death and sin (5:12-21), a life of rejoicing and righteousness is for the Christian not a mere fancy but a genuine reality (5:1-11). For example, the Christian is enabled to overcome sin (chap. 6); he is no longer under the law system that he could never fulfill (chap. 7); and he is set free from the dominion of sin and death in order to live a new life of righteousness and hope in the power of the Holy Spirit (chap. 8).

THE BENEFITS STEMMING FROM FREEDOM FROM THE WRATH OF GOD

5:1-11

Are there any benefits or fruits in the life that result from God's act of justifying us through faith? Paul relates that peace, joy, love, and hope mark the lives of those who have been justified before God (5:1-11). Finally, in a very difficult section at the end of chapter 5 (vv. 12-21), Paul portrays an analogy between Adam and Christ where the oppressive rule of sin, death, and the law is set over against the liberating dominion of righteousness, life, and grace.

Even though certain things are clear in this section and the next, it must be admitted that the precise flow of Paul's thought in this chapter is difficult. It is clear that positive blessings accrue to the justified, such as peace (v. 1), joy (exult, vv. 2, 3, 11), love (vv. 5, 8), and hope (v. 2). On the other hand, it is not clear what lies in the back of Paul's mind to evoke this emphasis. Perhaps he is thinking of an objector who doubts that the faith method of justification is safe after all. Can we really be sure, Paul, that God justifies sinners simply by faith? Such an attitude lurking beneath the surface of a person's mind could destroy any permanent rejoicing over a new status before God. In the "much more" expressions (vv. 9, 10, 15, 17, 20), Paul, in using the common argument from the lesser to the greater, appears to be trying to offset any feelings of *uncertainty* that his teaching may have produced.

PEACE

The first consequence of having been justified by faith is "peace with God" (v. 1). This peace is not first of all a psychological tranquility or peaceful feeling. Rather, this peace must be the experience of the factual status of a man who has been justified before God. It is the opposite of being under the wrath of God (1:18). Man's relationship to God has been altered in justification from one who is a rebel against the law of God to one who is fully acquitted, forgiven, and empowered to a new life. Peace depicts the consciousness of a new, deep personal relationship with God the Judge.[1] Of course, the inner contemplation of this objective fact can and should produce a real feeling of composure and security. Consider, for example, the results of being under the wrath of God as they are manifested in the life. We experience alienation from self and others, loneliness, and lack of purpose. Not to be any longer under the wrath of God should result in a positive consciousness of reconciliation with self and others and a meaningful reorientation to God's whole created order (2 Cor. 5:17). Such a peace distinctly alters our life. The thought of this kind of peace leads Paul eventually into a discussion of reconciliation (vv. 10-11).

GRACE AND JOY

On the basis of this new reality of justification, Paul can now speak of "this grace in which we stand" (v. 2). Being totally accepted by God through faith, the man of faith has continual peace with God—the cessation of hostility—and enjoys living constantly by God's grace. For Paul, grace encompasses not only the past free gift of forgiveness through the sacrificial death of Jesus (3:24), but also the whole present and future state of the believer. Such complete provision allows him to continually "exult." The past and the present having been thus secured, the Christian looks forward to the

1. Some Greek manuscripts at this point read: "*let us* have peace with God" (in the sense of "enjoy peace"). The change in one Greek letter in the word (*echomen* to *echōmen*) makes the verb "have" a hortatory-subjective instead of an indicative. It is difficult to settle the matter. The context strongly favors the indicative over the subjunctive (see John Murray, *The Epistle to the Romans*, p. 158; Anders Nygren, *Commentary on Romans*, p. 193; C. K. Barrett, *The Epistle to the Romans*, p. 101), although some argue that the third verb (exult in tribulations) in verse 3 favors the subjunctive idea based on an observation of actual Christian experience, and thus all three verbs should follow the mss. that read the subjunctive. Cranfield agrees and adds that this peace, or reconciliation, with God is the theme of the whole section (*A Critical and Exegetical Commentary on the Epistle to the Romans*, 1:255).

full manifestation of God's grace in the future; he rejoices in the "hope of the glory of God" (v. 2). The hope of glory comes before us further in chapter 8. Note well the nature of the new life. At the same time it is a life both present and coming, something at hand and a reality waiting for its future fulfillment.

Note here Paul's use of the interesting word "introduction" (v. 2). In Ephesians 3:12 the same Greek word is translated to give the picture of a worshiper gaining access to the holy place of God by means of a sacrifice. In nonbiblical literature the term can convey the thought of the admission of ambassadors to an audience with great kings (see 1 Pet. 3:18).[2] Our relation to Christ has gained for us this introduction to God's grace.

Following the Civil War, a dejected Confederate soldier was sitting outside the grounds of the White House. A young boy approached him and inquired why he was so sad. The soldier related how he had repeatedly tried to see President Lincoln to tell him he was unjustly deprived of certain lands in the South following the war. On each occasion, as he attempted to enter the White House, the guards crossed their bayoneted guns in front of the door and turned him away. The boy motioned to the soldier to follow him. When they approached the guarded entrance, the soldiers came to attention, stepped back, and opened the door for the boy. He proceeded to the libary where the President was resting and introduced the soldier to his father. The boy was Tad Lincoln. The soldier had gained an "introduction" (audience) with the President through the President's son.[3] How much more should we rejoice in our access to the grace of the King of kings!

2. TDNT, 1:132.
3. Abraham Lincoln, as cited by Donald G. Barnhouse, *God's River, Romans 5:1-11* (Grand Rapids: Eerdmans, 1958), p. 39.

HOPE AND SUFFERING

Christian rejoicing, however, is not directed only to the glorious future. Paul says, "We also [even] exult in our tribulations" (afflictions) (v. 3). We rejoice in the future hope of the glory of God, but we also rejoice in present trials. Why should trials be the occasion for joy in the Christian's life? Because they turn us away from trust in ourselves to "perseverance." But why is perseverance so valuable? Because perseverance, or endurance, is the attitude that looks beyond the immediate affliction to find its ultimate meaning in God (James 1:2-4).

Trials, rather than destroying our faith, actually develop a "proven character" (v. 4).[4] In a humbling type of experience, distresses turn us away from self-trust to complete trust in God. Our persevering attitude in trials brings glory to Him and thus a tried, or proven, character to us (2 Cor. 11:30; 12:9). When we are brought to the place where we have nothing else but God, we suddenly realize He is all we need. When we thus look totally to God as a result of the trials, we are assured of His approval; and that approval strengthens our hope in the glory of God (vv. 4-5). Andrew Murray has captured the thought:

> First, he brought me here, it is by His
>   Will I am in this strait place; in
>   that fact I will rejoice.
> Next, He will keep me here in His love,
>   And give me grace to behave as His child.
> Then, He will make the trial a blessing,
>   Teaching me the lessons He intends me to learn,
>   and working in me the grace He means to bestow.
> Last, in His good time He can bring me out again—
>   how and when He knows.

---

4. The Greek is *dokimē,* which means an object or person who is tested and shown to be reliable, trustworthy, valuable (see 1 Cor. 3:13; 1 Pet. 1:6). In Phil. 2:22 the same word refers to the "approved" or "qualified" (for missionary service) person of Timothy.

I am here (1) by God's appointment, (2) in His keeping, (3) under His training, and (4) for His time. Thus, faith, rather than being insecure because of trials, actually uses suffering to strengthen our hope in God's future glory. It is by suffering that hope is tested and strengthened.

LOVE OF GOD

Further, this hope will not prove to be misdirected hope ("does not disappoint," v. 5). We know this because we already have the foretaste of its consummation—"the love of God has been poured out within our hearts through the Holy Spirit who was given to us" (v. 5). The pouring out of the Holy Spirit seems to vividly recall Pentecost (Acts 2). The love that has been poured out and continues to grip us (Gk. *ekcheō,* to pour out like a stream) is not our love for God (Augustine) but God's love for us (vv. 6-8). The validity of our hope is attested by the experience of the overwhelming of our hearts by God's love. We are made aware of this love by the presence and activity of the Holy Spirit, who has been given to us at conversion (see John 7:37-39). This is Paul's first clear reference to the Holy Spirit in the epistle. Because everything in the Christian life depends on the Holy Spirit, Paul will develop this truth more extensively in chapter 8. He cannot leave this theme of God's love until he has said something further.

In verses 6-8 Paul elaborates on the nature of God's love, which is best described by what it does. The description offers clear proof that God loves men, sinful as they are. God's love is demonstrated chiefly in the cross: "Christ died for us" (v. 8). Paul is anxious to show us the unique nature of this love. God's love is totally unmotivated by any desirable qualities in the person loved. Paul calls us "helpless" (v. 6), "ungodly" (v. 6), "sinners" (v. 8), and even "enemies" (v. 10). While some men may evidence their love by giving their life for a just man (or cause), what is never heard of is a man dying for his enemy, yet this is precisely what Christ has done.[5]

In verse 9 Paul returns to the original thought of the paragraph, the benefits of justification. Since justification by Christ's blood is now a present reality—"We have peace with God" (v. 1)—the future is more than secured.[6] The "wrath of God" certainly refers to the future "day of wrath" and judgment of God (2:5). While salvation awaits its final consummation in the future, the evidence of God's love and grace shown in our present acquittal should more than assure us of future deliverance from the judgment of God.

Since parallel expressions are used in verses 9 and 10 for "justification" and reconciliation, we may assume they are different metaphors describing the same reality. However, the basic idea in reconciliation goes beyond justification and means "to reverse an unfavorable relationship between persons." Our relationship in sin before God constitutes us as "enemies" and requires the cessation of enmity and estrangement between us and God, or reconciliation: "If while we were enemies, we were reconciled to God through the death of his Son" (v. 10) refers to the past objective removal of the obstacle between God and man. The expression "much more, having been reconciled [justified], to God . . . we shall be saved by His [resurrection] life" refers to our acceptance of God's reconciliation and looks forward again with certainty, based on the evidence of the cessation of enmity, that we will through the life of Jesus be completely delivered from God's

5. The repetition in verse 7 seems redundant. There is no distinction here between a "good" man and a "righteous" man; both clauses express the same idea (Barrett, *The Epistle to the Romans*, p. 106; Murray, p. 167). See J. B. Lightfoot in Murray, p. 33, for the opposite view.
6. "Justified by His blood" (or at the cost of His blood) refers back to 3:25, where the emphasis is on the propitiatory nature of Christ's death. It is essential to the gospel to stress that Christ's life was poured out in death (blood) at the satisfaction for God's wrath against man's rebellion. Deemphasizing the blood aspect of Christ's death tends to eliminate the wrath aspect of God's judgment upon man and the real significance of the gospel.

final wrath (Rom. 4:25; Heb. 7:24-25). Note that Paul always links our whole relationship to God (past, present, future) with Jesus Christ.

Verse 11 simply repeats the thought of verse 10 and adds Paul's note of rejoicing in the fact that we who believe in Jesus now possess this reconciliation.[7] Probably this idea of reconciliation, more than any other Paul has used, stresses that in justification there is a reversed relationship to God. Relationship to God affects the whole life of man (Col. 1:20, 22; Eph. 2:16). For a Christian, a whole changed life results from his faith response to God's love gift in Christ (2 Cor. 5:19-21). Can we do otherwise than rejoice in this whole new situation of reconciliation?

ADAM AND CHRIST

5:12-21

This passage (vv. 12-21) is generally recognized to be at the same time both the most profound and the most difficult in the whole book of Romans—if not the whole New Testament. Some see the section as an abrupt, unrelated, and generally unintelligible insertion into Paul's main argument. Others strongly insist it is the high point of the whole epistle, in the light of which the whole is best to be understood.[8] Some have also charged, perhaps justly, that it is precisely at this point in

---

7. It is significant to note that Paul says we have *received* the reconciliation. There is a difference between the English word reconcile and the Greek term (*katallagē*). In English, to speak of reconciliation as effected means that both parties (offended and offender) are mutually reunited. On the other hand, while the Greek word may also denote this same idea (see 1 Cor. 7:11), it may also convey the thought of a one-sided process where the obstacle to fellowship has been removed and the objective reconciliation offered to the offender. God is not Himself reconciled but removes the obstacle to fellowship (God's holy wrath against man's rebellion) in the death of Jesus and now offers to sinful men this reconciliation as a free gift through faith (2 Cor. 5:17-19). For this view see TDNT, 1:255ff. On the equally defensible view of dual reconciliation, see Leon Morris, *Apostolic Preaching of the Cross,* pp. 186ff.

8. Nygren, p. 19.

the book of Romans where evangelical theology, in failing to sustain interest, has weakened its position.[9]

The master thought of the whole passage revolves around the concept of two representative headships (Adam and Christ) and two consequent groups of mankind, where each person is linked solidly to each other and to their respective heads. This explains Paul's constant use of the word "one," as in "one man" (v. 12), "one who sinned . . . One, Jesus Christ" (vv. 16-17), and so on. The point to grasp is that Paul is viewing man's condition of fallenness (under condemnation), as well as his condition of being saved (acquittal), not first of all as an individual matter but, in the one instance as well as in the other, as a matter of being *in* a representative (1 Cor. 15:22, 45-49).

Christ has a tremendous historical significance. When Adam departed from God, because he was the representative head of the whole human race, his act was not something that concerned only him as an individual. In Adam's act of disobedience, sin and death became universal in the whole historical human order. On the other hand, through Christ, the new representative man, in the same all-inclusive way and even more so, life has become universal in the historical human order. Death in the Bible is not simply the termination of all bodily functions. Physical death ensues because of our sinfulness and ultimately negates and condemns human life. It is death indeed because man dies as he has lived—in a state of rebellion against his Creator and in alienation from his fellowman.

Life, on the other hand, is not the mere continuation of bodily functions. Instead, life follows from the gift of God's grace (righteousness, acquittal) through relationship with Jesus Christ. It is life indeed because of the blessedness in this human life of being freed from the slavery of sin and death (Heb. 2:15), and because it leads on into the goal of an eternal life in this same blessedness.

9. Adolf Schlatter, cited in ibid.

Our solidarity with our fellows is a reality we often overlook in the assertion of our individuality. John Donne's oft-quoted words eloquently express the truth of human oneness:

> No man is an island, entire of itself; every man is a piece of the continent, a part of the main. If a clod be washed away by the sea, Europe is the less, as well as if a promontory were, as well as if a manor of thy friend's or of thine own were: any man's death diminishes me, because I am involved in mankind, and therefore never send to know for whom the bells tolls; it tolls for thee.[10]

If we ask whether human nature can ever be changed, Paul might answer, no and yes. In Adam the race can never be changed. But a new humanity has come to birth: the old "Adam-solidarity" of sin and death has been broken up and replaced by the new "Christ-solidarity" of grace and life. However, at the present time these two humanities overlap in the individual life of a Christian. Those who were formerly in Adam, even though now in Christ, still bear the sentence of bodily death belonging to Adam's race. But those who are in Christ have assurance that they have received from God that justification which brings resurrection life in its train.

Underlying the whole passage (vv. 12-21) may be the question of how the one man, Jesus Christ, in His death and resurrection could provide such a universal and certain hope of salvation. The subject of the reconciliation of mankind in verses 10-11 has perhaps stirred the question. Paul's answer lies, strangely, in appealing not to the deity of Christ, but to His perfect humanity. Jesus was representative man in *obedience* to God as Adam was representative man in *disobedience* to God. If the first man, Adam, could bring the whole race (in him) into sin and death by one act of disobedience, likewise (more so!) the Son of man, the last Adam, could bring the whole race (in Him) to acquittal and

10. John Donne, *Devotions upon Emergent Occasions* (Ann Arbor, Mich.: U. of Michigan, 1959), pp. 108-9.

life by one act of righteousness (death on the cross).

In verses 12-14 Paul first emphasizes the headship of Adam. It may be seen in the following diagram:

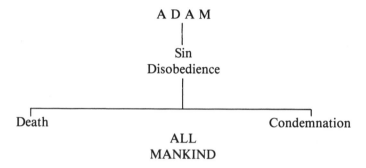

A D A M

|

Sin
Disobedience

|

Death   Condemnation

ALL
MANKIND

In passing, we may remark on the historicity of Adam, a debated subject in our day. If we insist on the necessity of not the mere idea of a representative in Christ but the actual, historical figure of the man Jesus as essential to the gospel, can we then eliminate the need for an actual, historical man, Adam, in favor of the idea of a mere symbolical representative? Can the idea, rather than the actual historical reality, form the valid counterpart to the necessary reality in Christ's actual, historical significance? We believe it essential to Paul's argument that the first representative man, Adam, was as historically real as the last representative man, Christ.

Paul's expression stating the cause of universal death is: "because all sinned" (v. 12). Considerable discussion has developed over the years about the correct sense of this expression. Some argue that we all die because we all sin individually, as did Adam (Pelagian view).[11] But this explana-

---

11. The "for that" of the KJV is *eph ho,* which means "because" (NASB, NIV). The Vulgate translation "in whom" (*in quo*) is a mistranslation but may reflect a true interpretation (F. F. Bruce, *The Epistle of Paul to the Romans,* p. 130). The "as" at the beginning of the section (v. 12) anticipates the completion of a comparison in a "so." The comparative "so" never seems to come. The sense, though, is clear from v. 19, where the "as" is repeated and followed with a "so" in a summary of the whole section.

tion fails to account for why we all choose to sin and why infants still die who do not voluntarily sin. Others argue that Paul clearly intends that we see a definite connection between the sin and death of Adam and the sin and death of us all (vv. 13-15, 19). There are three main variations of this second view. The *first*, the Augustinian, understands that we all sinned "in Adam" in the sense that we were seminally in Adam when he sinned, and thus in a sense we did what he did (cf. Heb. 7:4-10). More popular is the view that "because all sinned" refers to our "solidarity" with Adam, and therefore the "all sinned" of verse 12 refers to the same events as the "one trespass" of verses 15-19—that is, the "Fall of Adam" (federal headship view). A *third* variation of this same emphasis sees "all have sinned" (v. 12) to refer to all men's actual personal sinning but as a result of their connection to Adam and his sin (contrast this with the Pelagian view above). We all sin in our turn and die as a result, because we all inherit Adam's corruption. Although it is difficult to decide between variation two and variation three, we will follow the latter in the following exposition.[12]

Even in the absence of any specific divine commandments from the time of Adam to the time of Moses universal sinfulness is evidenced, even though sin as violation of a revealed command was not imputed to men. Sin was still universally and pervasively present among mankind and was death-inflicting (vv. 13-14). These verses most naturally support the view adopted above (v. 12), which understands that all men were corrupted in Adam's act of disobedience. Paul adds that Adam was a "type" of the one who was to come (i.e., Christ). Perhaps the word *analogy* would better suit Paul's use of the word "type," if understood as an historical counterpart. "In both cases the act of one man has far reaching consequences for all other men. It is not necessary that the ways in which the consequences follow from the acts

12. Murray, p. 186; Bruce, p. 130; Nygren, p. 214. See also Russell Shedd, *Man in Community* (Grand Rapids: Eerdmans, 1964), especially chap. 3.

should also be exactly parallel."[13] There really can be no adequate parallel to Christ, but Adam is the closest.

In verses 15-19 Paul sets forth in comparison and mostly by contrast the headship of Christ to that of Adam. Diagrammed, it might look like this:

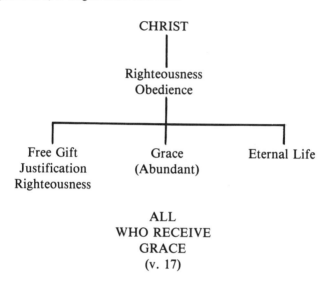

CHRIST

Righteousness
Obedience

Free Gift	Grace	Eternal Life
Justification	(Abundant)	
Righteousness		

ALL
WHO RECEIVE
GRACE
(v. 17)

Throughout, Paul goes out of his way to emphasize the fact that God's grace in Christ operates more inclusively and more intensively than Adam's sin and condemnation. He can only keep saying, "much more," "abounded," "abundance" in reference to Christ's work for man (vv. 15, 17, 20). Those who are touched by Adam's transgression are much more touched by one Man's act of righteousness.

Verse 17 is an important and beautiful verse. It refers to two governments, or systems (death and grace), under which all men live: "Death reigned through the one, . . . those who receive the abundance of grace and of the gift of righteousness will reign in life" (v. 17). Man's chief problem is that he

13. Cranfield, 1:278-79.

lives under the oppressive dominion of both personal sin and a corporate system of sin. Both dominions produce in him the fear of death. But through the "abundance of grace and of the gift of righteousness" (v. 17), he can be released from captivity and enter into a whole new existence of acquittal and life in the man Christ Jesus.

This life is available only to those who "receive" the gift (v. 17). In this way Paul recalls all he has taught about the indispensability of faith (chap. 4). The entire passage (vv. 12-21) neither teaches universalism[14] nor strict individualism but representationalism with individual responsibility. We got into the mess not by individual decision alone but by relationship to our old head, Adam; we get out of the mess not by individual decision alone but by relationship to our new head, Christ. Note well how Paul teaches emphatically the necessity of faith response or "receiving" this grace in order for justification and life to come to us.

In verses 18-19 Paul continues the contrast between Adam and Christ with the use of the words "all men" and "the many." Again the problem of universalism arises. But Paul's thought is that in Adam's trespass all men actually came under condemnation, whereas in Christ's righteous act[15] all men provisionally come under acquittal, but only actually when they by faith receive God's gift (2 Thess. 1:8-9). The "many" of verse 19 could refer to the "all" of verse 18, but

14. Universalism is the teaching that ultimately all human creatures of God will be saved through the universal redemption of Christ. Rom. 5:18 and 1 Cor. 15:24-28 are especially appealed to for support of this teaching. Religious liberals, such as Nels Ferre, and some neoorthodox theologians, such as Karl Barth, have in recent days advocated on different grounds the ultimate salvation of all men. See Bernard Ramm, *A Handbook of Contemporary Theology* (Grand Rapids: Eerdmans, 1966).

15. The Greek is *dikaiōma,* "righteous act" (TDNT). The same word occurs also in 5:18 as well as 2:26; 8:4. "Paul means not just Christ's atoning death but the obedience of his life as a whole" (Cranfield, *Romans,* 1:289).

the expression "the many" refers to a group solidarity in a way that "all" men does not (Rom. 12:4; 1 Cor. 10:17). Probably this latter fact guards the biblical doctrine of acquittal from the error of universalism since only those who are in the "group" solidarity participate in the results of the representative's act. Only those who by obedient faith are in "the many" of Christ's headship participate in being constituted righteous before God (Mark 10:45).

But Paul, haven't you forgotten the most important historical event of all, the dispensation of the law? How does this affect salvation-history? At this point his answer is simple and to the point (later in chap. 7 a more elaborate answer is given): "The Law came in that the transgression might increase" (v. 20). Law "slipped in" (Gk. *parerchomai*) as an inferior part of God's chief plan (i.e., the promise, Rom. 4; Gal. 3:19). Sin is revealed in all its fullness as rebellion only in the presence of divine law. Actually, law does not remedy the sin problem, it aggravates and even increases it (7:5-11). But the increase of sin through the law cannot defeat God's grace because: "Where sin increased, grace abounded all the more" (v. 20). Finally, the main threads of the section are summed up in verse 21 by contrasting the rule of sin through the tyranny of death with the new rule of grace through righteousness (acquittal before God), which leads to eternal life through (only through) the Lord Jesus Christ.

To summarize this section (vv. 12-21), we note that our forefather, Adam, as the first *representative man,* plunged the whole human posterity into sin and death. From such a predicament mankind could not of itself escape. On the other hand, as a result of the appearance of the second and last *representative Man* and His unmitigated obedience to God, even to His propitiatory death, there emerged a radically new humanity. This was possible because Jesus was from the beginning the incarnate Son of God. As a man He totally surrendered Himself to God, even to death, in order that life which was peculiarly His as the obedient, incarnate Son (i.e., eternal life) might spring forth to all His posterity.[16]

The human condition of man in sin in the world can indeed be changed, but not by human action—only through divine intervention. Each element in this chapter converges upon the other to guarantee through God's grace the certainty of both the present love of God to us and our future security against any powers that would threaten to annul our eternal salvation. In the light of such certainty, anything less than continual rejoicing is a mockery of God's truth.

16. "Eternal life" is that distinctive *quality* of the life that was manifested in the human life of Jesus Christ (see 1 John 1:2). It is eternal in its *quality*, first of all, rather than its duration (though it does go on forever), since it is the incarnate life of Jesus Christ. This emphasis keeps us from separating eternal life from the present experience. Although it is future in one sense, it is also *now* in part in another sense (see John 5:24).

5

THE NEW SITUATION: FREEDOM FROM SIN'S CAPTIVITY
6:1-23

Paul's main argument and thesis of the letter is finished. He has advocated that all are under condemnation as rebels against God, but the Creator has intervened on behalf of all by providing acquittal and forgiveness for them through the substitutionary death of Jesus (1:18—3:31). Furthermore, he has stated that this acquittal before God comes to us individually irrespective of our moral virtues or lack of them. Acceptance before God comes solely by faith that trusts in the God who reveals Himself and who has acted for our salvation in Jesus' death and resurrection (4:1-25). Lastly, he has described the grounds whereby we may be continually rejoicing in assurance of our future salvation (5:1-11). Again, such certainty rests not on our moral accomplishments (law keeping), but solely on the grace of God (5:12-21). Paul even teaches that as sin increases, grace increases the more (5:20).

It is at this point that the apostle moves perilously close to the edge of an abyss—one step to the side and all that he has gained by what has preceded can be lost. For it would be easy to conclude, if we have understood Paul clearly, that, if the law is subordinate, and if grace is more manifested as sin increases, there is no reason for Christians to be morally good. Why not go on sinning that the supply of grace might be increased (v. 1)? Will not God be the more glorified because our continual sin will continually manifest His grace? This is the antinomian (complete moral freedom) error that misunderstands Christian freedom and unfortunately has been present in every era of Christianity, including today's. The grace of God in Jesus Christ is indeed freedom (Rom. 6:15-18; Gal. 4-5), but freedom *from* sin, not freedom *to* sin (1 Pet. 2:16).

A notable historical instance of the abuse of Paul's teaching can be seen in the Russian monk Rasputin, the evil genius of the Romanov family in its last years of power. Rasputin taught and exemplified the doctrine of salvation through repeated experiences of sin and repentance; he held that, as those who sin most require most forgiveness, a sinner who continues to sin with abandon enjoys each time he repents more of God's grace than any ordinary sinner.

In Paul's day, the form of the argument that abused the doctrine of justification took two twists. Paul devotes the lengthy section of chapters 6 through 8 to answering these two objections. The first is an ethical objection introduced by the question, "Are we to continue to sin that grace might increase?" (6:1). This is answered in 6:2-14 by Paul's appeal to the reality in the believer's life of a radical inner change witnessed to in baptism and consisting in the fact of the believer's crucifixion and resurrection with Christ.

The second objection is more of a legal problem, introduced likewise by a question in 6:15: "Shall we sin because we are not under law, but under grace?" Paul answers this distortion by first appealing to the true nature of Christian freedom, namely, captivity to righteousness (6:15—7:6); second, by showing the true function of the Mosaic law (7:7-25); and third, by illuminating the nature of the life of freedom in the Spirit in chapter 8. These are the most important chapters in the entire New Testament for establishing that the Christian life is continual moral renewal and progressive holiness (sanctification).

UNION WITH CHRIST IN HIS DEATH AND RESURRECTION

6:1-14

The charge (v. 1), it may be recalled, was to the effect that since more sin calls forth more grace (5:20), shall we not go on sinning to get more and more grace? Paul's first reaction is abhorrence—"May it never be!" (v. 2).[1] Then he states that such a conclusion embodies an inherent contradiction: "How shall we who died to sin still live in it?"[2] At the outset we can note that this fact of the Christian having died to sin is the fundamental premise of the whole argument in the chapter. The "who" of the verse is a specialized Greek form (*hoitines*) that gives this paraphrased sense: We who in our essential nature are Christians (acquitted in Christ), *we* have died. Death and life are not compatible. To be a Christian means to have died to sin. Therefore, it is a fundamental moral contradiction for a Christian to be still living in the sin to which he has died.[3]

But how did we die to sin? To answer this question, Paul uses three metaphors. He first appeals to the importance of our death to sin in the metaphor of Christian baptism. Certainly the truth of their death to sin was known to all the Christians at Rome: "Do you not know?" Yet how much of its real significance did they actually know? It may be difficult to know exactly where Paul depends upon common knowledge and where he goes beyond popular understanding to the fuller implication. But we may assume that they at least knew that to be "baptized into Christ Jesus" was equivalent

1. See note 35 of chapter 2.
2. The rendering "dead to sin" (KJV) misses the force of the definite past tense of the indicative verb by giving the effect of a status of death rather than the specific past event of conversion. The NASB, NIV's "died to sin" is preferred. Cranfield distinguishes four different senses in which Christians die to sin, and corresponding to them, four different senses in which they are raised up: (1) died to sin in God's sight (*juridicial sense*, v. 2); (2) died to sin in their baptism (*baptismal sense*, v. 3); (3) die to sin daily by the mortification of their sinful natures (*moral sense*, v. 11); and (4) will die to sin finally and irreversibly when they actually die—and just as finally and irreversibly at Christ's coming, when they will be raised up to the resurrection life (*eschatological sense*, vv. 5b, 7) *A Critical and Exegetical Commentary on the Epistle to the Romans*, 1:299-300).
3. To "live" in sin suggests not occasional sin but to have sin as the moral atmosphere that our lives breathe (E. H. Gifford, "Romans," in *The Bible Commentary:* New Testament, 3:125).

to the fuller expression to be "baptized into the name of Jesus Christ" (Matt. 28:19; Acts 2:38; 10:48; 19:5).

To be baptized into the name of Christ meant to be baptized (placed) into union with Jesus Christ. To be baptized into Moses was to come under the authority of Moses' leadership and to be a participant in all the privileges that included (1 Cor. 10:2). To be baptized into the name of Paul meant to be baptized into the discipleship and dedication of Paul, an idea that Paul passionately rejected (1 Cor. 1:13, 15). Hence, baptism into Christ means baptism into union with Him, into dedication to Him, and into participation in all that Christ is and has done. Now if baptism means that Christians are united to Christ, it means first of all that we are united with Him in His death; that is, to use a second metaphor, we are co-crucified with Him (v. 6).

Furthermore, our union with Christ means that not only are we identified with Christ to the extent that we are "buried with Him through baptism into death" (v. 4), but in the same manner we are also united to Him in His resurrection (vv. 5, 8), so that now we might walk (conduct ourselves) in a new (resurrection) life (v. 4).[4] This new quality of resurrection life is later pointed out to be a kind of life that is lived in full obedience to the glory of God (v. 10).[5]

Paul proceeds in verse 5 to reinforce this fact that to be united with Christ means to participate both in His death and also in His resurrection life: "For if we have become united

---

4. The assumption of many to the effect that Paul has in mind by the use of the word "buried" the immersionist mode of baptism is not necessarily warranted. There does not seem to be similar imagery in the uses of "united" (fused) (v. 5) or "crucified" (v. 6). Baptism itself signified full identification with Christ in His death to sin. One could see baptism as immersion if water baptism signified *only* death (under the water) and not also resurrection. Such may actually be the case.

5. From this point onward Paul drops the figure of baptism and speaks directly about our identification with Christ's death and resurrection. One of the major assumptions about baptism upon which these verses depend is that baptism is always linked closely with the conversion experience (faith in Christ), not as the efficacious element in justification, otherwise Paul would have dealt with it in chapters 3-5 (see Acts 10:48;

with Him [Gk. *symphutoi,* grown together] in the likeness of His death, certainly we shall be also in the likeness of His resurrection" (v. 5). The words "grown together" and "likeness" are very difficult to understand. This third metaphor, "grow together," may be understood in the sense of a tree graft. Again, the figure used stresses vital joining, or fusing.

But does "likeness of His death" refer to baptism or to the actual death of Christ? Probably neither. It signifies neither complete identity (that which is) nor mere similarity (that which is similar to), but a very close likeness (that which is precisely like). So it refers neither to water baptism nor to the death of Christ itself, but rather to the spiritual transformation that takes place at conversion when we become united with a death to sin precisely like Christ's. It is not required that we should die the actual physical death of Christ, but to die as Isaac did in the similitude and figure of his death; that is, to die to sin. Thus also the expression "We shall be also in the likeness of His resurrection" does not necessitate now an actual physical resurrection like Christ's but simply shows that the value of our union with Him now in His resurrection makes possible the distinctively new life of the Christian. The "likeness of His resurrection" is the "newness of life."[6]

It seems that Paul has in mind in these verses *both* the inward reality of death to sin and the rite of water baptism. Water baptism, however, should be viewed in the context of

1 Cor. 1:18), but more as the seal or symbol of the righteousness given by faith (see 4:11). A true symbol is not the reality itself but points to something beyond itself as the actual reality. But there is a sense in which a symbol participates to some extent in the reality to which it points. Water baptism is the symbol that points to the already established reality of the codeath. While some argue for just Spirit baptism in this passage (W. H. Griffith-Thomas, *Commentary on St. Paul's Epistle to the Romans* [Grand Rapids: Eerdmans, 1946]), almost all commentators understand Paul to be referring only to water baptism. Probably *both* are in view. See the excellent discussion of this passage in James D. G. Dunn, *Baptism in the Holy Spirit* (Naperville, Ill.: Allenson, 1970), pp. 139-51.

6. Gifford, p. 127.

the early church, where it was the means of expressing one's faith in Jesus Christ. As such the reality and the rite are closely linked. However, it is also clear in Paul's teaching that it is faith-response to the gospel that effects the reality of salvation, and not the rite itself (1 Cor. 1:17).[7]

More specifically, "our old self was crucified with Him" (v. 6). The old self refers to the whole unregenerate man as seen in Adam: man's lifestyle under the rule of sin and death, judgment and condemnation (5:12-14). Under this figure the radical and comprehensive nature of the changed life situation of the Christian is highlighted (Gal. 2:20; 2 Cor. 5:17). Such co-crucifixion took place for the purpose that "the body of sin might be done away with" (v. 6). The "body of sin" does not refer to the human body as such. It either refers to the individual human body in its old condition as a slave of sin[8] or, more broadly, it means the old race solidarity of sin and death that all share in Adam.[9] In either case, the emphasis lies in the distinctively new life into which we have been introduced through Jesus Christ.

This old condition was "done away with" (v. 6). The Greek verb for "done away with" is *katargeō,* meaning "to make completely inoperative" or "to put out of use." The very purpose, then, of being so united to Christ in His death is to bring about our freedom from the slavery of sin. Paul views this from the analogy of being slaves to the master of sin in our old condition, "he who died [with Christ] is freed [Gk. *dikaioō,* 'justified' or 'acquitted'] from [the] sin [master]" (v. 7)[10]

---

7. George R. Beasley-Murray, *Baptism in the New Testament* (London: Macmillan, 1962), pp. 271-73.
8. Gifford, p. 128.
9. F. F. Bruce, *The Epistle of Paul to the Romans,* p. 139.
10. Some see here (v. 7) a reference to a general maxim that men are no longer liable for supposed sins committed after their actual death (H. P. Liddon, *An Explanatory Analysis of St. Paul's Epistle to the Romans,* p. 111). Paul, however, speaks of our spiritual death to sin with Christ in baptism (Cranfield, 1:311).

Does this imply that Christians no longer can or do sin? Experience would answer an emphatic no. Paul also recognizes that bonafide Christians (justified ones) may in fact sin (1 Cor. 1:2, 9, 11; 3:1-4; 5:5; 6:11). What Paul is teaching is that the desirability and necessity of sin have been broken. The Christian *may* sin, but the fact is that he no longer *must* sin, because this power of the sinful human life in Adam is annulled.

But how can the broken power of sin over our lives be actually realized in our day-to-day experiences? Is the Christian life merely a negative activity of ceasing to do things we formerly practiced? Paul answers these questions by focusing attention on the positive side of our union with Christ. This is really the answer to the crucial question posed in verse 1 of why Christians should lead a moral life. In thinking of the death of Christ, our attention is immediately focused also on the historical counterpart of that death, the resurrection of Jesus.

In verses 8-10 the apostle describes the kind of death Jesus died and the kind of resurrection life He now lives. Jesus "died to sin, once for all" (v. 10). Christ died once for all to the power of sin over his life. It is not that He Himself sinned, but in His total identification with us as sinners on the cross, He experienced the power of sin ruling over Him and bringing Him to death (2 Cor. 5:21; 1 Pet. 2:24). He died once in obedience to God, yet under sin's power in order that He might break the power of sin's enslavement over our lives (8:3). Now Christ raised from the dead lives a life totally for God only. He lives in complete obedience—He never lived otherwise—to God, yet without facing the prospects of sin and death ever again. So Christians who died this kind of death (once for all victory over the power of sin) also share with Christ in this new life (totally for God, of willing obedience to Him). If this is true, any suggestion that faith-righteousness leads us to continue living in sin and disobedience is entirely contrary to the facts of our new relationship to Christ.

But this victory over sin in the life is not an automatic process. Paul states that we must continually (present tense) "consider yourselves to be dead to sin [as an enslaving power], but alive to God in Christ Jesus" (v. 11). The practice of victory over enslaving sin comes not by trying harder or by self-abnegation, but by "considering." This is the same word used to describe God's "reckoning" righteousness to Abraham by faith (4:3). "In Christ Jesus" we are newly related to God. This new relationship has put us in an entirely different position to the formerly enslaving sin. When a solicitation to do evil (to disobey God) confronts us, we are to count on the fact that we are now in Christ, part of a new humanity that is freed from the old captivity that led us to follow sin's dictates. Chrysostom (d. A.D. 407) expressed the moral challenge in the memorable line: "If then you died in your baptism, stay dead!" Furthermore, we are alive with Christ's resurrection life to serve in obedience to God. Christ's victorious death to sin's power is also our victory; Christ's resurrection to continual life and obedience to God is also our new life.

But, one may sigh, after all, Paul, aren't we still human? Don't we live in a world full of lust and evil desires? Paul answers in verses 12-14 with exhortations based on the truth he has established in verses 1-11. The "lusts" (Gk. *epithumiais,* desires) are the values that lead us away from obedience to Christ (v. 12). They are the grave clothes that are carried over from the former life to the new. Specifically, they are the habits of sin learned in the old Adamic lifestyle. We must fight and rebel against sin's rule, because we are "as those alive from the dead" (v. 13). For the Christian, life is a great paradox. He is dead to sin but still lives with it; he is alive with Christ, yet still in the mortal body; he is fully righteous by God's justification, but still a sinner needing to progress into full obedience to God in sanctification (v. 19). The Christian lives between two ages. He is called upon to live now in the old age as if the new age had already come ("as those alive," v. 13). In reality, the believer through justification already participates in the future glory in Christ.

The key to this new life lies in: (1) "considering" (v. 11) and (2) "presenting" (v. 13). To "present" (Gk. *paristanō*) means to place at the disposal of another for service. As Christians, we are to stop offering our members (such as eye, hand, foot) to sin as "instruments" against God for establishing unrighteousness. Rather, we are without delay to abandon our whole beings to God as alive in the resurrection life of Jesus and to offer our bodily members to God as weapons against evil for establishing righteousness (v. 13). Needless to say, the continual, moment-by-moment presentation of our bodily members to God can only be done after we have unreservedly presented our wills to Him. This distinction is reflected in the translation where the two different Greek tenses Paul uses for the two occurrences of the verb "present" in verse 13 are handled differently.[11]

In verse 14, Paul states that sin will not lord it over us because we are "not under law, but under grace." What does it mean to be not under law but under grace? Although there are different views,[12] Paul probably does not have in mind the Christian's release from the moral nature of the commandments (which he is arguing against), but freedom from the law as a system of both justification and striving after ethical goodness (sanctification). The law system causes sin to be strengthened and multiplied (5:20), because it offers nothing but condemnation to its violaters (4:15; 7:10) due to the weakness of sinful human flesh (8:3). Hence, to be under law

11. There is a play on the Greek tenses in the two occurrences of "present" in v. 13. In the first instance the present tense is used with the negative. The sense is "stop presenting." In the second instance the Greek aorist tense is used with the effect of an immediate decisive, and final act: "abandon yourself at once forever." It should also be noted that "righteousness" as Paul uses the term in this verse carries with it the rarer idea in Paul of ethical goodness.

12. At least four prominent views can be identified: (1) not under the law's *authority;* (2) not under the law's *condemnation* of sinners; (3) not under the law's *justification* for obedience to it; and (4) not under the law's *contractual obligations* (see Richard N. Longenecker, *Paul, Apostle of Liberty,* pp. 145-48). Good interpreters hold all four of the views (see Cranfield, 1:319-20).

is to be under enslavement to sin, because law aggravates sin
and condemns the sinner, and yet in itself it has no power to
deliver the transgressor. More of this later (7:1ff.).

Grace, on the other hand, stands for the whole delivering
power and virtue of Christ's death and resurrection and our
union with Him in that death and resurrection. Grace was
manifested to remove us from the enslavement to sin by providing all that we need to serve God in obedient love. Do we
see, then, how contradictory it is to ask whether we should
live in sin that grace may abound?

BONDAGE TO RIGHTEOUSNESS

6:15-23

Although the moral problem of freedom from law is picked
up more specifically in 7:1-6, Paul does begin in a general way
to answer this obvious difficulty. He has just stated that we
are free from the law and under grace (6:14). An objector
might say, Well, if that's the case, Paul, can we not ignore the
law and sin (violate law), since the law no longer is over us?
Again Paul answers the question as before (v. 2), with an emphatic "may it never be!" (v. 15). This response clearly shows
that to be free from the law does not mean to be indifferent
toward God's moral will. Freedom from law is not freedom
to sin. Without God's moral law, man loses the ability to
recognize the seriousness of sin. Law may be powerless to prevent sin, but God's commands at least ensure that sin will be
taken seriously. Since God's law reveals His will, the Christian can never be indifferent toward it. There is a sense in
which the Christian is not under law and another sense in
which he is (Rom. 13:8-10; 1 Cor. 9:21). In our day of moral
relativism, it is especially important to listen carefully to
Paul's teaching. More on this later (13:9-10).

In verses 16-23, Paul describes Christian freedom as bondage, or enslavement, to the will of God (righteousness). He
employs the natural analogy ("human terms," v. 19) of the

slave-master relationships to press home his point.[13] When a person presents himself willingly in obedience as someone's servant, he then becomes exclusively *that* master's servant and no one else's (v. 16). The slave-master analogy is quite appropriate, since no one could be the slave of two different masters at the same time. The nature of slave precludes it. Jesus said, "No man can serve two masters . . . You cannot serve God and Mammon" (Luke 16:13; see John 8:34). In a man's heart (religious center of human existence), only two options are available for his obedience. A man chooses as his master either sin or God. To choose to be free to follow one's own desires is actually to chose sin as master (v. 12). Sin leads ultimately to eternal death; obedience to God leads to eternal life (v. 23).

Paul is confident that the Romans have responded to that "form of teaching" (or pattern of teaching) preached in the gospel concerning obedience to God through Jesus Christ (v. 17). Note that the gospel came to them with definite content, because they became "committed" to it (Rom. 6:17; 1 Cor. 15:3).[14] We see from Paul's mention of this "form of teaching" that the gospel was not Paul's only; it was the common Christian message. The good news not only freed them from captivity to sin, but it also enslaved them to their new master, righteousness (v. 18). They were freed from sin to be servants of God and righteousness (ethical goodness, in this context).

Paul continues his exhortation to the effect that we should no longer put our bodily members at the disposal of impurity (serving one's passions), leading to more and more wicked-

13. This is certainly Paul's point in verse 19 when he says, "I am speaking in human terms," or in human illustration.
14. Actually the verb is passive in voice and second person plural. The NASB correctly renders: "to which [pattern of doctrine] you were committed." They were delivered to the teachings of the Word of God, which created them in Christ and ruled their life. It is still true, however, that this body of truth was also delivered unto them (see 1 Cor. 11:23; 15:3; 2 Thess. 3:6).

ness (moral indifference), but to offer those bodily members to the disposal of righteousness (the will of God) for "sanctification" (v. 19). The term "sanctification" (Gk. *hagiasmos,* better: "sanctifying") is part of a word group in the New Testament including the words "holy," "saint," "purify," "hallowed," and "holiness." It means first of all to be set apart wholly for the use, or service, of God. Secondly, it means to acquire, because of this relationship, certain moral qualities of the one to whom we are set apart. Sanctification proceeds from justification, as fruit from the vine, and never justification from sanctification (i.e., the tree from the fruit). The process of sanctification is the work of the Holy Spirit, and Paul will develop this in chapter 8.

Finally, the passage stresses again the contrast between obedience to sin in the former non-Christian life and obedience to God (vv. 20-23). The service done for sin and the service done for God each produces its own reward, or fruit, and also its own end (final) product. Sin's fruit consists in things of which the Christians are now ashamed and leads ultimately to (eternal) death (v. 21). God's fruit, on the other hand, consists in sanctification (ethical goodness) (Rom. 6:19; Gal. 5:22-23) and ultimately leads to eternal life (v. 22). To sum up, Paul states that the old sin master (life in Adam, 5:12-14) pays the ultimate wages of death.[15] Sin is a deceiver; it offers life and ends up paying death. As the "wages" are a continuous process, "death" may be thought of as not only the ultimate pay, but also as casting its shadow back into the present existence. On the other hand, the free gift of God (not wages) offers finally eternal life in Jesus Christ our Lord (v. 23), which also casts its shadow back into this life.

So the new rule of grace through justification by faith leads not to a life lived in sin but to a new life with Christ in the service of righteousness (God's will). The rule of sin under the

---

15. The Greek *opsōnion,* wage or pay, used especially for military service as a *bare* allowance (TDNT); see Luke 3:14; it was used also for slaves (Moulton and Milligan).

law system that enslaved men has now been broken and replaced by the rule of grace. But the Christian takes sin
seriously because grace, rather than freeing us to be servants
of our own sinful passions, has instead enslaved us to God
and His righteousness, with the result of fruitful service and
ethical sanctification.

The keynote, then, for the Christian life is single-minded
obedience to God's will revealed in Jesus Christ our Lord.
The controversial German theologian Dietrich Bonhoeffer
has written some noncontroversial words about this *costly
grace:*

> Cheap grace means the justification of sin without the justifi-
> cation of the sinner . . . who departs from sin and from whom
> sin departs. Cheap grace is *not* the kind of forgiveness of sin
> which frees us from the toils of sin. Cheap grace is grace
> without discipleship, grace without the cross, grace without
> Jesus Christ, living and incarnate. Costly grace is the grace of
> Christ Himself, now prevailing upon the disciple to leave all and
> follow Him. When he spoke of grace, Luther always implied as
> a corollary that it cost him his own life, the life which was for
> the first time subjected to the absolute obedience of Christ.
> Happy are they who, knowing that grace, can live in the world
> without being of it, who, by following Jesus Christ, are so
> assured of their heavenly citizenship that they are truly free to
> live their lives in this world.[16]

But what about this matter of the law (6:14)? How did we
get from law rule to righteousness rule? What about the law
then? Isn't it a bad deal after all? Why was the law given? We
must hear Paul further in chapter 7 for these answers.

---

16. Dietrich Bonhoeffer, *Cost of Discipleship,* p. 47.

6

THE NEW SITUATION: FREEDOM FROM THE LAW'S DOMINATION

7:1-25

This chapter continues to answer the objection that to be under the rule of grace and not law is to be indifferent toward sin. Paul has already answered this objection in one aspect by showing that the Christian is free from sin only to be a slave of God and righteousness (6:15-23). Previously Paul has simply made assertions about the law: "Now we know that whatever the Law says, it speaks to those who are under the Law, that every mouth may be closed, and all the world may become accountable to God; because by the works of the law no flesh will be justified in His sight; for through the Law comes the knowledge of sin" (3:19-20); "Do we then nullify the Law through faith? May it never be! On the contrary, we establish the Law" (3:31); "the Law brings about wrath; but where there is no law, neither is there violation" (4:15); "the Law came in that the transgresson might increase" (5:20); "Shall we sin because we are not under law but under grace?" (6:15).

Paul's statements about the law seem to contradict one another. On the one hand he obviously takes the law (that is, the Jewish law as contained in the Old Testament) to be the definitive expression of God's will for the ordering of human life (2; 3:31). On the other hand, he maintains that the law does not enable man to escape the sinful and earth-oriented existence in which he finds himself (3:20; 4:15; 5:13, 20).

Chapter 7 provides some clues in reconciling these apparent opposite polarities.

The history of the controversy over the function of the law in the Christian life is long and varied. Luther viewed the law as playing only a two-fold negative role: (1) Its *civil* function is to restrain sin by threatening punishment, and (2) its *theological* function is to increase sin, especially in the conscience, and show man how corrupt he actually is. Calvin, on the other hand, attempted to synthesize gospel and law and saw its primary purpose for the Christian as *didactic,* or *instructional,* to help him understand God's will and excite him to obedience. Paul Althaus, a contemporary German theologian, has in recent days suggested another thesis. He understands the New Testament to teach that God's loving commands that express His desire for our fellowship have through the fall become law, and as such are negative and prohibitive rules that condemn man. Yet through the gospel the same law is transformed once again into the loving commands of God. In this sense he would concur with Calvin that the Christian is free from legalism but not from the commands.[1] Not to clarify this distinction between law and legalism can lead to two extremes: (1) modern legalism or (2) pure license in the name of "freedom."

Today the relationship of the law to Christian ethics has received renewed interest because of the popular teaching of the situation ethicists, who maintain that the only absolute norm for the Christian is love. To the situationist, such as Joseph Fletcher, to be governed by the norm of divine commands is legalism. According to him, if I determine that love (as I understand it) is better fulfilled by setting aside one or all of the divine norms in any given situation, I am at liberty and must set them aside.[2] Since the apostles rejected moral

---

1. Paul Althaus, *The Divine Command,* trans. Franklin Sherman (Philadelphia: Fortress, 1966). A short but helpful Lutheran treatment of the law before and after conversion.
2. Joseph Fletcher, *Situation Ethics* (Philadelphia: Westminster, 1966). A popular treatment of the viewpoint.

lawlessness (1 John 3:4-6), the question of the Christian's relationship to the standard of God may be crucial in understanding who are authentically Christ's disciples today.

The Marriage Analogy
7:1-6

The question of why sin will not enslave us because we are under grace and free from the law (6:14) comes to the fore. It is for Paul the most important and yet the hardest point in his extended discusson. First, the general truth is stated that it is the nature of law (of any kind) to have power over a person only as long as he lives (v. 1). For example, the law of marriage (either Jewish or Roman) binds two people together as long as both are alive. But if the husband (or wife) dies, the law that binds the two in marriage is canceled, and in this case the widow is no longer under obligation to the law of marriage. She would be legally considered an adulteress if, while her husband was alive, she was to join herself to another man; but, when her husband is dead, she is no longer bound by the law and may marry another (vv. 2-3).

Thus far this is all Paul has said. His point is not to teach for or against divorce in this context. He simply wants to illustrate the fact that in commonly accepted terms, death sets aside marriage law obligations.

But what does it mean? We should not attempt to press Paul's analogy into a full allegory (where every part has an analogous counterpart), otherwise it will not be completely appropriate. In the application of the analogy that he gives in verse 4, the Christian corresponds to the woman in the illustration, and the law to the husband. As the law binding a woman to a man is set aside by the man's death, so the law to which men formerly owed allegiance is set aside through our dying with Christ. A death having taken place allows a new marriage to ensue (i.e., to the risen Christ). Whereas we were formerly bound by the law (of Moses), now we have been "made to die to the Law through the body of Christ,"[3] and we are free to be united to another Lord, "even to Him who was raised from the dead." The thought parallels chapter 6:5-8 and Galatians 2:19-20: "For through the Law I died to the Law, that I might live to God. I have been crucified with Christ; and it is no longer I who live, but Christ lives in me." Why was death to the law necessary? So that the "fruit" of the Spirit might spring forth (vv. 4, 6).

Why was the law not able to bring life and fruit for God? Because before we were Christians ("while we were in the flesh"[4]), the passions or impulses connected with sins were aroused in us through the law (v. 5). These passions used our bodily members to produce thoughts and acts characterized by death. It is the same idea that Paul developed in 6:20-22, with the added connection in this context between law and sin. Such was our condition—outside of Christ and grace. "But now" (v. 6) that we are Christians, married to the resurrected Christ, we have been released (v. 2) from the Mosaic law that held us captive. "Newness of the Spirit" (v. 6) is a reference to the Holy Spirit (chap. 8), who effects the newness of life in service to God; while the "oldness of the letter" refers to the legalistic approach to the written tables of the law (2 Cor. 3:4), which were powerless to effect a righteous life before God because in the context of the whole law system they brought condemnation. But how or in what sense did the law of God hold us "bound"? (v. 6).

Paul with some of his Jewish contemporaries had believed

---

3. Bo Reicke offers help in the difficult elements of the analogy when he suggests that instead of Paul having one idea in mind, two different motifs become blended in the argument: the Law that has died to the Christian and the Christian who has died to the Law. (JBL LXX [1951] 267. Cited by Richard N. Longenecker, *Paul, Apostle of Liberty*, p. 146).

4. Paul uses "in the flesh" (Gr. *sarx*) in two different senses, depending on the context. Christians are in the flesh in the sense of being in the mortal body (2 Cor. 4:11; 10:3; Gal. 2:20; Phil. 1:22, 24); yet they are no longer in the flesh in the sense of being dominated by sin, death, and law (Rom. 7:5; 8:9; Gal. 3:3; 5:24).

that in the keeping of the law was found the only way to acceptance and peace with God (Deut. 4:1; 6:25; Rom. 7:10). As a legalist in pursuit of God's justification, he attempted to keep the strict legal observances of the whole law (Phil. 3:6). Now Paul views the law as God's standard, but also in a negative fashion as arousing sin (5:20; 7:8) and leading a person to death and condemnation (7:9, 10; 2 Cor. 3:7, 9). Why had his view of the law been so radically reversed? The only adequate answer lies in his confrontation with the risen Lord on the Damascus Road and his acceptance of Jesus as the Christ of God (Acts 9). The law had been fulfilled by Jesus.

But how did this change his view of the law? Something like this: Jesus was alive! This meant that God had accepted Him, and the curse of the cross was not Jesus' own but ours (Gal. 3:10-13). Paul had kept the law blamelessly, yet he had agreed in the justice of the crucifixion of the young Nazarene carpenter! He kept the law (he thought) and yet was still the "chief of sinners," because he persecuted those who believed on Jesus as the Messiah (1 Tim. 1:13, 15). The law then had not made him righteous before God, because he had misappropriated it as the occasion for sinful boasting in his own goodness. The law had worked just the opposite effect in Paul from what he had supposed. Instead of making him righteous before God, it really had condemned him. How then does sin pervert the right use of the law?

THE TRUE NATURE OF THE LAW

7:7-25

Actually Paul found in his experience that the law which promised to promote life instead provoked sin in him, and as sin increased death ruled. How so? When the law was originally given to Israel at Sinai (Ex. 20), it also offered the promise of life for those who did the law (Deut. 4:1). Yet in Paul's view, "if a law had been given which was able to impart life, then righteousness [acquittal and life] would indeed have been based on law [of Moses]" (Gal. 3:21). But something is wrong. The big problem is that all men are transgressors of the law (Gal. 3:22). Life, under the system of law, was only guaranteed to those who fulfilled perfectly the requirements of God's commands (Gal. 3:12; Lev. 18:5).

To break the law in one point was to be a transgressor of law, and no transgressor of law could receive life on the basis of lawkeeping (James 2:10). The effect of breaking one of the commandments of the law is not like the effect of breaking one of the bristles on a broom, where we can go on sweeping pretty well even with broken bristles. The effect of breaking a commandment is more like that of breaking a pane of window glass; break it in one place and you shatter the whole glass! God does not grade on the curve! For breaking the law, the "curse" of the law fell on life (Deut. 11:26-28; 27:26; 28:15-68).[5]

Paul interprets the curse of the law as ultimately involving condemnation and eternal death (Rom. 5:15, 18). Under such a law-principle of justification, our condition was hopeless. But God intervened through Christ, who, though He was born under the law, was not condemned by it because He fulfilled it (Matt. 5:17). Therefore, when Jesus died, He bore the curse of the law in His own body for us (Gal. 3:13). God took the condemnation that the law brought to us because of our violations and nailed it to Jesus on the cross (Col. 2:14; 2 Cor. 5:21; 1 Pet. 2:24). So in Christ's death we died to the slavery of the law's condemning finger, and we now serve God through the Spirit without any fear of condemnation for violating one of God's commands (8:1).

Wasn't the law, then, actually a bad thing ("sin," v. 7)? Paul's answer is emphatically no—"may it never be!" "The

5. The law consisted also in a gracious provision for forgiveness of sins through the sacrificial ceremonies (Lev. 1-7). When an Israelite had sinned in violation of the law, his sin could be atoned for by the offering of a blood sacrifice. But God's purpose for the moral law remained the same until the coming of Christ (Gal. 3:21-22; Heb. 9:24-25; 10:1). The latter verse in Hebrews reminds us that the law did contain a "shadow" of good things to come in the gracious sacrificial system that pointed toward Christ.

Law is holy, and the commandment is holy and righteous and good" (v. 12). He must steer a close course between the twin perils of legalism and moral indifference to divine law. On the one hand Paul affirms emphatically there is nothing wrong with the law ("spiritual," v. 14), yet the law proves in experience to be powerless to rescue a man from his sinful predicament. The problem is not the law; it is the sinful nature it has to work on that is the culprit. Even a Rembrandt is powerless painting on tissue paper. Can we blame the anchor if the boat drifts when anchored in loose mud?

In verses 7-13 Paul seizes on the tenth commandment, "coveting," to illustrate how the holy command working on the sinful nature of man actually produces "coveting of every kind" (v. 8). Sin uses the good command as an "opportunity." The Greek work (*aphormē*) is often used in military and commercial contexts to denote the base of operations for an expedition or a war.[6] Sin launched an attack against man and viciously and deceptively used the commandment as a foothold for the advance.

When a harmless balloon filled with warm water is brought near a coiled rattlesnake, the snake strikes out at the heat and releases its poisonous venom into the balloon. Until the balloon is presented, the poisonous venom lays dormant in the glands of the snake, but the balloon provides the "occasion" for the release of the poison into plain view. Similarly the law, while good in itself, has the effect of drawing out the poison of man's sin into deliberate acts of rebellion against God. In Bunyan's *Pilgrim's Progress,* the pilgrim, Christian, is taken by Interpreter into a large room (the heart) full of dust (sin). A man (law) comes to sweep with a broom, causing the dust to rise up so much that Christian is almost suffocated.[7]

6. W. F. Arndt and F. W. Gingrich, *Greek-English Lexicon of the New Testament,* s.v. "*aphormē.*" Käsemann reminds us that in Jewish tradition the tenth commandment was the core and summary of the law (*Commentary on Romans,* p. 194).

7. John Bunyan, *The Pilgrim's Progress*, new ed. (New York: Dutton, 1954), pp. 31-32.

Verses 7-12 describe Paul (and all of us) either in his boyhood experience or in his experience as a Pharisee afflicted with guilt. When a Jewish boy becomes old enough to assume his own responsibility for the commandments (*Bar Mitzvah*), he may discover also a new desire to enter into the prohibited world upon which God has placed what seems to him to be an unwarranted restraint.[8] Thus, in attempting to keep the commands of God, he dies in the experience of disillusionment and disappointment. For instead of receiving life through the commands, he experiences death because he cannot find the power to perform the commandment and is thus separated from his Creator (vv. 9-10). But Paul hastens to emphasize that the fault lies not with the commandment, because it is a true expression of God's will, but with the sinful nature of man that takes the good command and through it brings death to us (vv. 11-12). Sin through the command is revealed in all its rebellious character (v. 13). Like an x-ray photograph, the law reveals the cancer of sin within us. Truly the law is "spiritual" in that it comes from the Spirit of God and is a true expresson of His will (v. 14). God's law came that we might recognize sin (3:20; 7:7).

We have deliberately avoided until this point the chief interpretive problem of this chapter, which has produced numerous divergent views. Here is the problem. When Paul uses the first person singular *I* (vv. 7-25) and the present tense (vv. 14-25), is he referring to his own experience as an unregenerate man under the law or to his experience as a Christian? While the question of when this experience occurred is not really Paul's main point,[9] it has deeply bothered Christians from the earliest times to the present. In a lecture

---

8. Paul's references to "coveting" (lust), "commandment," "life," "death," and "deceived" in these verses are strongly suggestive of the whole account of man's original fall into sin recorded in Gen. 3. Cranfield downgrades the *Bar Mitzvah* explanation and argues that Paul is describing mankind's experience before the giving of the law (*A Critical and Exegetical Commenatry on the Epistle to the Romans,* 1:351).

9. Paul's main point is to answer the charge that his teaching about not being under law makes the law sin (v. 7).

on Paul's description of himself as being "sold under sin," Dr. Alexander Whyte said,

> As often as my attentive bookseller sends me on approval another new commentary on Romans, I immediately turn to the seventh chapter. And if the commentator sets up a man of straw in the seventh chapter, I immediately shut the book. I at once send the book back and say, "No thank you. That is not the man for my hard-earned money."[10]

It is also possible to take "I" in verses 7-13 to speak of Paul the unregenerate man (and unregenerate men) and the "I" in verses 14-25 of Paul the regenerate man (and regenerate men). (Barrett, Murray, and Cranfield following Calvin.) This seems to be the best position.

If we dismiss the less likely position that Paul's "I" in verses 14-25 is merely a general reference to mankind or the Hegelian progress of history view of Stauffer,[11] there are three possible interpretations: (1) Paul (and all of us), the non-Christian Pharisee under the law (Greek fathers, Sanday and Headlam), (2) Paul (and all of us), the normal Christian (Augustine, Bruce, Murray), and (3) Paul (and all of us), the carnal Christian (W. H. Griffith-Thomas). Although it seems impossible to us to adopt any one of the three views without some dissatisfaction, we will discuss and argue for the second view. No doubt the reason there is no unanimity among commentators on this point of interpretation is that the passage relates a psychological experience, and depending on our own pre-Christian and Christian experience, we will lean toward interpreting Paul's experience in accord with our own.

In favor of view number one are the expressions in the passage that are felt to be incompatible with the Christian state: "I am of flesh, sold into bondage to sin" (v. 14); "but I practice the very evil that I do not wish" (v. 19); "making me a prisoner . . . Wretched man that I am!" (vv. 23-24). In

10. Cited by F. F. Bruce, *The Epistle of Paul to the Romans,* p. 151.
11. TDNT, s.v. *"ego."*

favor of view number two are the expressions thought to be incompatible with a non-Christian experience: "I joyfully concur with the law of God" (v. 22); "I myself with my mind am serving the law of God" (v. 25); "the good that I wish" (v. 19). In favor of view number three is the fact that the person described seems to desire the good and hate the evil, but he lacks the power to overcome evil and ends in despair (vv. 18, 24). Since there is no reference to the Holy Spirit in chapter 7 (except possibly verse 6), it is obvious to those who argue for this third view that Paul describes himself as a Christian who is trying to live for God in the power of the flesh by law conformity. Thus, in the mind of those who feel the section describes the carnal Christian, Paul's main point is the inability of the law in itself (i.e., as a total *system*) to effect fruit unto God.

In our view the main confusion in interpretation has arisen because of attempts to force a chronological or logical sequence on Paul's experience from chapter 7 to chapter 8 rather than seeing the two chapters as complementary. It is precisely because it is Paul's real experience that all the difficulty has arisen. We have lost the point of his teaching by getting overly involved in the precise time when he experienced this despair. It is the truth of the continual presence of sinful nature in the redeemed man that the apostle seeks to describe. When one gets to chapter 8, indeed the picture changes with the emphasis on the life of the power of the Holy Spirit. Yet this new emphasis in chapter 8 is not designed to deny that every Christian experiences to some extent throughout his life the feelings of chapter 7. Paul in chapter 8 gives the complementary and simultaneous experience in our lives (Cranfield).

It is clear that there is a conflict, or battle, described in verses 15-25 that does not appear in verses 7-13. Paul also changes tenses at verse 15, using the past tense in verses 7-14 and then the present in verses 15-25. Might this not suggest that the first section (vv. 7-13) deals with Paul's past, unregenerate experience under the law and corresponds to the words in verse 5, "while we were in the flesh . . . to bear fruit for death," while from verse 15 onward he is describing the way the sinful nature operates within him as a redeemed person who desires to do the good? The same conflict (vv. 15-25), hardly possible in one who has *died* (vv. 9, 11), is described by Paul in Galatians as a conflict in the Christian between the Holy Spirit and the sinful flesh (Gal. 5:17).

He is burdened throughout the whole section to show that the law is good (v. 12) but powerless because of the sinfulness of man. His inward conflict proves the spirituality of the law. It is not until verse 25, which anticipates the resurrection life, that there is any indication of hope beyond the sorry experience in the chapter. Perhaps a few comments on words and meanings in verses 14-25 will help to draw this tedious discussion to a fruitful conclusion.

In verse 14, "of flesh" means fleshy and hence weak, sinful, and transitory.[12] "Sold into bondage" (literally, under sin) refers to the captivity produced in us by sin working through the good law (see also v. 23). "I do not understand" (Gk. *ginōskō*) of verse 15 reveals that Paul is perplexed by the strange way the law works on his sinful nature: he cannot practice what he desires (the law of God). Instead the apostle ends up doing what he hates, which proves that he agrees in his conscience that the law is good even though he does not do it (v. 16).

The contrast between "I" and "sin which indwells me" in verse 17 should not be made the basis for any profound psychological theory. The statements should be understood as popular terms to describe Paul's personal conflict, and not a technical development of a particular theory of psychology.

In verse 18 the sense of the last clause is helped if we read: "but the *power* to perform the good is not." Verses 21-23 contain several references to "law." "The law of God" (v. 22) and "the law of my mind" (v. 23) are definite references to the Mosaic law. "The principle" (v. 21) and

---

12. Arndt and Ginrich, p. 751.

"the law of sin" (v. 23) refer to a type of counterfeit law, or principle, operating in the sinful flesh that makes war on the true law of God and takes a man captive to do its evil bidding. In verse 23 the expression "making me a prisoner" refers to making military prisoners in the sense that sin, warring against God's will in my life, wins the victory and through law makes me a prisoner (see Luke 4:18; Eph. 4:8; 2 Cor. 10:5). Recent prisoner of war experiences in Viet Nam make this image more meaningful to our day.

"Wretched man" (v. 24) is Paul's wail of anguish; it is a very strong term of misery and distress. "The body of this death" (v. 24) refers to the human body that through sin and the law has fallen under the dominion and condemnation of death. Paul's misery is due to a frustrated condition but not a divided self. He wants to serve God totally with his innermost redeemed self (vv. 15, 19, 21, 22, 25), but he finds his desire frustrated by the irrationality of his actual performance. He cries out for release from the sinful nature. As Tennyson, in *Morte d'Arthur,* cried, "O for a new man to arise within me and subdue the man that I am." But where can such release be found? Paul knows the answer because he writes as a Christian: "Thanks be to God [release comes] through Jesus Christ our Lord" (v. 25). In another place Paul uses the exact same expression as a reference to the future bodily resurrection of the dead at Christ's return (1 Cor. 15:57). Ultimate release from this perpetual frustation comes through the future redemption of the body (8:23). Meanwhile, the present work of the Holy Spirit in the believer, which anticipates in a small measure the glorious future deliverance, enables him to partially rise above the weaknesses of the sinful flesh and live unto righteousness (chap. 8).

If the logical or chronological interpretation has been stressed in verses 14-24, the last part of verse 25 will be out of place. If Paul was indeed moving toward a conclusion in the chapter that would prepare his readers for an entirely new emphasis in chapter 8, he most certainly would have ended on the triumphant note of 25a. But he closes the discussion by giving what appears to be his present experience: "I myself with my mind [inward man, his spirit] am serving the law of God, but . . . with my flesh [I serve] the law of sin." By ending thus, he emphasizes that even he himself as a Christian in this world cannot escape the frustrations of living a new life in Christ in a body which, until the resurrection, still bears the marks of the old Adamic race. But chapter 7 is not the whole story of Christian experience.[13]

13. For a recent and quite convincing attempt to argue view no. 3 on p. 106 (Paul, the fleshly Christian) see David Wenham, "The Christian Life: A Life of Tension?—A Consideration of the Nature of Christian Experience in Paul," chap. 6 in *Pauline Studies,* D. A. Hagner and M. J. Harris, eds. (Grand Rapids: Eerdmans, 1980). Also for the view that Paul's experience under the law was not negative or guilt-ridden, see Krister Stendahl, "Paul and the Introspective Conscience of the West" in his *Paul Among Jews and Greeks* (Philadelphia: Fortress, 1980), pp. 78-96.

SELECTED BIBLIOGRAPHY

Since good commentaries on Romans abound, it may be more helpful to list some worthy volumes in several categories, with brief comments, than to multiply titles. Unless otherwise noted, the writers are conservative in theology.

BROAD OVERVIEW AND SYNTHESIS

Erdman, Charles. *The Epistle of Paul to the Romans.* Philadelphia: Westminister, 1925. Best for summarizing the overall content of each section and tracing the logical argument. Not verse by verse.

Liddon, H. P. *An Explanatory Analysis of St. Paul's Epistle to the Romans.* Grand Rapids: Zondervan, 1961. Excellent on the logical point-by-point progression, in outline form with notes. Quite detailed and technical. Good historical material.

Ridenour, Fritz. *How to Be a Christian Without Being Religious.* Glendale: Gospel Light: Regal, 1967. Very popular treatment involving *The Living Bible* paraphrase with general comments in modern language, with illustrations. Not much depth, but a good, light introduction to Romans.

Spivey, Robert A., and Smith, D. Moody, Jr., *Anatomy of the New Testament.* Rev. ed. New York: Macmillan, 1974. Not a conservative book, but highly commendable for putting the chief content of Romans into historical perspective for more advanced students.

Stifler, James M. *The Epistle to the Romans.* Reprint. Chicago: Moody, 1983. Good on tracing the thought progression and general content. More detailed than Erdman above.

EXEGETICAL AND INTERPRETIVE

Barrett, C. K. *The Epistle to the Romans.* New York: Harper & Row. 1957. Not thoroughly conservative, but close to the biblical text and one of the best in this category.

Bruce, F. F. *The Epistle of Paul to the Romans.* Grand Rapids: Eerdmans, 1963. Good treatment of almost all verses, with help in the area of historical illustration materials.

Cranfield, C. E. B., *A Critical and Exegetical Commentary on the Epistle to the Romans.* The International Critical Commentary. 2 vol. Edinburgh: T. & T. Clark, 1975, 1979. The best more-detailed critical study available in English. For advanced students. A rich mine of interpretive help.

Gifford, E. H. "Romans." In *The Bible Commentary: New Testament,* vol. 3. Edited by F. C. Cook. New York: Scribner's, 1895. Old and out of print, but still one of the best careful treatments of the thought and details.

Käsemann, Ernst. *Commentary on Romans.* Grand Rapids: Eerdmans, 1980. Scholarly, highly technical, and not conservative, but contains a wealth of exegetical and historical material for the advanced student.

Mickelsen, Berkeley. "Romans." In *Wycliffe Bible Commentary,* Charles F. Pfeiffer and Everett F. Harrison. Chicago: Moody, 1962. An excellent brief exposition and interpretation by a leading evangelical scholar.

Murray, John. *The Epistle to the Romans.* 2 vols. Grand Rapids: Eerdmans, 1959. Easily one of the best treatments on the book. Careful, evangelical, and detailed.

Nygren, Anders. *Commentary on Romans.* Philadelphia: Fortress, 1949. A powerful treatment of the epistle by a Lutheran theologian. Very helpful on main argument of book. Not thoroughly evangelical.

Palmer, Earl F. *Salvation by Surprise: A Commentary on the Book of Romans.* Waco, Tex.: Word, 1975. A fresh interpretation with emphasis on theological interpretation and contemporary thought.

PAULINE THEOLOGIES

Bruce, F. F. *Paul: Apostle of the Heart Set Free.* Grand Rapids: Eerdmans, 1977. Some feel this is the best work this prolific evangelical British scholar has produced. Quite readable.

Longenecker, Richard N. *Paul, Apostle of Liberty.* Grand Rapids: Baker, 1976. This is an earlier but brilliant and seminal study on the background and chief theological emphases of Paul.

Ridderbos, Herman. *Paul.* Grand Rapids: Eerdmans, 1975. A massive, penetrating, and comprehensive examination of Paul's theology by one of the leading conservative New Testament scholars in the Netherlands.

OTHER SUGGESTIONS

Jones, Alexander, gen. ed. *The Jerusalem Bible.* New York: Doubleday, 1966. Produced by Dominican Catholics in Jerusalem and containing in Romans, with a few exceptions, some excellent notes and fresh insights on the text.

Kittel, Gerhard and Friedrich, G., ed. *Theological Dictionary of the New Testament.* Translated by Geoffrey W. Bromiley. 9 vols. Grand Rapids: Eerdmans, 1964. An unabridged English translation for advanced students with some Greek background. Rather heavy, but when used with theological discrimination it is a valuable resource for interpreting Romans. (Referred to in the text and notes of this book as TDNT.)

Brown, Colin, ed., *The New International Dictionary of New Testament Theology.* 3 vols. Grand Rapids: Zondervan, 1975. This is a similar but smaller work like Kittel's above but done by conservatives. Highly recommended.